COCKTAIL CHEMISTRY

NICK FISHER

PHOTOGRAPHY BY AUBRIE PICK

COCKTAIL CHEMISTRY

The ART and SCIENCE of DRINKS from ICONIC TV SHOWS and MOVIES

SIMON ELEMENT

NEW YORK   LONDON   TORONTO   SYDNEY   NEW DELHI

SIMON
ELEMENT

An Imprint of Simon & Schuster, Inc.
1230 Avenue of the Americas
New York, NY 10020

First Simon Element hardcover edition May 2022

SIMON ELEMENT and colophon are trademarks of Simon & Schuster, Inc.

For information about special discounts for bulk purchases, please contact Simon & Schuster Special Sales at 1-866-506-1949 or business@simonandschuster.com.

The Simon & Schuster Speakers Bureau can bring authors to your live event. For more information or to book an event, contact the Simon & Schuster Speakers Bureau at 1-866-248-3049 or visit our website at www.simonspeakers.com.

Photography Copyright © 2022 by Aubrie Pick
Drinks Stylist: Amanda Anselmino
Prop Stylist: Glenn Jenkins
Photo Assistant: Nathaniel Yates Downes

Interior design by Matt Ryan

Manufactured in China

1 3 5 7 9 10 8 6 4 2

Library of Congress Cataloging-in-Publication Data
Names: Fisher, Nick (Mixologist), author. | Pick, Aubrie, photographer.
Title: Cocktail chemistry: on-screen drinks recreated and reimagined / Nick Fisher; photography by Aubrie Pick.
Identifiers: LCCN 2021039137 | ISBN 9781982167424 (hardcover) | ISBN 9781982167455 (ebook)
Subjects: LCSH: Cocktails. | Cocktail Chemistry (YouTube show) | LCGFT: Cookbooks.
Classification: LCC TX951 .F524 2022 | DDC 641.87/4—dc23
LC record available at https://lccn.loc.gov/2021039137

ISBN 978-1-9821-6742-4
ISBN 978-1-9821-6745-5 (ebook)

TO MY WONDERFUL PARTNER, RISHITA,
WHOSE ENDLESS SUPPORT AND
ENCOURAGEMENT ENABLED COCKTAIL
CHEMISTRY TO GROW FAR BEYOND WHAT
I EVER IMAGINED POSSIBLE.

CONTENTS

INTRODUCTION

I STILL REMEMBER THAT DARK 'N STORMY COCKTAIL FROM 2008. IT WAS LIKE NOTHING I'D EVER TASTED BEFORE.

With a complex ginger kick and a mild rum funk, it was a perfectly balanced drink that I kept thinking about on the taxi ride home from the newly opened Clover Club bar in Brooklyn. I was in my early twenties and suddenly found myself in the heart of a New York City cocktail renaissance, which planted the seed for my love of craft cocktails. After moving to the East Village in Manhattan and frequenting legendary downtown cocktail bars like Death & Co, PDT, and Pegu Club, I was hooked.

I continued my quest after moving to San Francisco, but these cocktails weren't easy on the wallet. I started to wonder if one could recreate those fifteen-dollar Old Fashioneds at home, and with a little trial and error, I was able to hack together a passable replica. Then a gift from my partner, Rishita, changed everything. It was a "Cocktails 101" class at a famous local speakeasy called Bourbon and Branch. I'll never forget showing up solo to an event that was clearly designed for couples on a date.

I awkwardly took my seat for one at the bar, surrounded by couples making small talk, meaning the bartender instructor then had 100 percent of my attention. In that class I learned some key fundamentals of cocktail making: how to balance a drink with sugar and acid, the importance of fresh ingredients, and that there are really only a few foundational cocktail templates to learn.

Once I mastered the basics, I moved on to more elaborate experiments, often involving manipulation of ice. My "ice ball cocktail" (see page 147) was a ridiculous trick I created where I inject a cocktail into a hollow ice ball shell then smash it open for guests. After enough requests to explain how to make it, I filmed a low-budget video of the process on my smartphone and posted it to YouTube. Somehow that video took off, and Cocktail Chemistry was born in my kitchen!

Playing around with cocktails developed into a passion, which evolved into a YouTube channel, which resulted in the book you're holding today. I've never worked as a professional bartender, but through rigorous home experimentation, studying the science of flavor and balance, and no shortage of immediate (and often harsh) feedback from an online audience of hundreds of thousands of cocktail enthusiasts, I've developed a unique perspective on home bartending.

We home bartenders are growing in numbers every day, and with so many quality spirits, ingredients, and bar tools now on the market, there's never been a better time to go beyond your whiskey on the rocks or gin and tonic.

My YouTube channel has been designed for the home bartender and to meet you where you are in your cocktail journey, from classic recipes to advanced techniques. But I believe cocktails should also be about

having fun, and that inspired the structure of the channel. In that spirit I started recreating drinks from pop culture as a fun callback to iconic drinks, such as the Vesper martini from *Casino Royale* or butterbeer from *Harry Potter*, also improving on the original versions when needed (which is very often!).

This book follows the same format. Each section starts with a cocktail I recreate from pop culture. From there we explore related recipes and techniques, like how to make the ultimate martini or how to infuse bourbon with brown butter. These pages represent the culmination of the knowledge I've gained, both learning and teaching the craft of cocktails, and I couldn't be more excited to share it with you here.

Cheers,

Nick

BAR TOOLS

FOR THOSE JUST GETTING STARTED, HERE'S A BRIEF OVERVIEW OF STANDARD HOME BAR EQUIPMENT AND HOW IT IS USED.

1 BOSTON SHAKER

My preferred type of shaker; it either comes as two metal shaker tins or a combination of one tin and one pint glass. The latter version is heavier but tends to separate more easily after shaking. Shake drinks in a Boston shaker with four ice cubes to mix, chill, dilute, and aerate your cocktail, typically one with citrus juice. To learn more about how to shake a cocktail, see Shaken or Stirred? The Science of Dilution on page 30.

2 HAWTHORNE STRAINER

Use this coiled strainer with a Boston shaker to strain out large chunks of ice or other solids, such as fruit. After shaking the cocktail, hold the Hawthorne strainer firmly on top of the larger shaker tin when pouring the cocktail into your glass.

3 FINE-MESH STRAINER

This is a tool that allows you to "double strain" your cocktail by catching any finer bits from the shaker tin, such as citrus pulp or small shards of ice. Pour the cocktail through a Hawthorne strainer over the fine-mesh strainer directly into the serving glass.

4 COBBLER SHAKER

A common beginner's shaker, this three-piece set consists of a single tin with a cap on top and a built-in strainer that fits snugly on the shaker tin. The cap also doubles as a small jigger for measuring liquid ingredients. While the cobbler shaker might seem like an elegant all-in-one tool, the cap often sticks after shaking and the parts can be harder to clean than the ones in a Boston shaker.

5 MIXING GLASS

An optional tool for stirred cocktails, a mixing glass is typically used to make spirit-forward drinks with no citrus juice. While you can get away with just using a pint glass, I'd recommend investing in a proper mixing glass if you plan to make multiple stirred cocktails at a time. To learn more about how to stir a cocktail, see Shaken or Stirred? The Science of Dilution on page 30.

6 JULEP STRAINER

Originally designed to hold back ice from your mustached face as you sip your juleps and cobblers, today this strainer that looks like a large, perforated spoon is often cast aside in favor of the coiled Hawthorne strainer. I tend to use the julep strainer for stirred drinks in my larger mixing glass, but that's just a personal preference.

1

2

3

7 JIGGER

Essential for measuring liquid ingredients, jiggers come in all shapes and sizes and have different uses. Double-sided jiggers are efficient for bartending as they let you quickly pour to the surface of either the small or large end and dump the liquid into your mixing vessel.

8 BARSPOON

A long-handled spoon used primarily for stirring cocktails, the barspoon's thin and threaded shaft makes it easier to grip and manipulate than a conventional spoon. Recipes sometimes call for a barspoon of liquid, and while barspoons may vary in size the capacity of the spoon is typically about a teaspoon or 5 milliliters.

9 PEELER

A vegetable peeler is often used to shave a wide strip of zest from citrus fruit to create a "twist" for garnishing a drink. I prefer a Y-shaped peeler, occasionally trimming the twist with a knife to make the edges straight if I'm feeling fancy.

10 HAND JUICER

One of the most important tools for making sour cocktails with fresh citrus juice, a two-handled hand juicer is the easiest way to squeeze juice from lemons or limes. Invest in a high-quality durable juicer if you plan to make a lot of shaken cocktails.

11 METAL SPOON STRAW

Completely optional, but I love serving highballs or drinks in a Collins glass with this utensil. The bowl at the end of the straw makes it easy to mix the drink, and it's a more sustainable alternative to disposable plastic straws, which don't hold up nearly as well.

12 MUDDLER

A muddler is helpful for getting out all your pent-up rage as you extract juices or essential oils from fruits, vegetables, or herbs in your cocktail shaker. You can find a cheap wooden muddler or invest in a plastic-tipped metal version that's easier to clean.

13 SILICONE ICE CUBE TRAY (1.25-INCH CUBES)

While you can certainly use whatever ice cubes you have in your home freezer, I prefer making 1.25-inch cubes of ice in a silicone tray. They present better than those half-moon-shaped ice cubes from a plastic tray. I also use these cubes for shaking and stirring cocktails to achieve consistent chilling and dilution. Just be aware that over time the silicone can take on some freezer-burn taste that requires you to wash it.

14 SILICONE ICE CUBE TRAY FOR LARGE ICE CUBES (2-INCH CUBES)

This tray creates ice cubes that are large enough to be used for cocktails served in rocks glasses. Compared to multiple smaller cubes, large cubes have less surface area that won't dilute your drink as much. To learn how to make beautiful, perfectly clear ice cubes, see Clear Ice on page 54.

15 ICE BALL MOLDS (2.5-INCH)

These molds yield large ice balls that are perfectly spherical. Ice balls serve a similar purpose to large ice cubes (less dilution in your cocktail), but they are spheres.

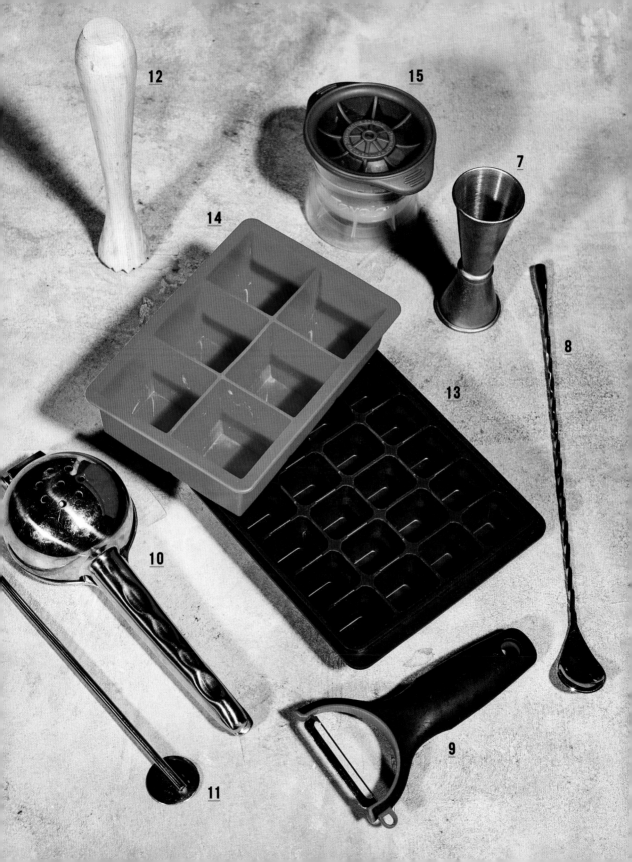

GLASSWARE

COCKTAIL GLASSES VARY BY
CAPACITY AND SHAPE, MAKING EACH
OPTIMAL FOR CERTAIN TYPES OF
DRINKS, BUT AT THE END OF THE
DAY IT LARGELY COMES DOWN TO
PERSONAL PREFERENCE. WANT TO
DRINK YOUR OLD FASHIONED OUT
OF A SOLO CUP? HAVE AT IT. HERE
ARE SOME OF THE MORE COMMON
TYPES OF COCKTAIL GLASSWARE AND
WHAT TO SERVE IN THEM.

1 OLD FASHIONED GLASS

Sometimes called a "rocks glass," it's short and wide and often used for cocktails served, you guessed it, "on the rocks" (meaning over ice). You'll use it all the time for spirit-forward or sour cocktails. The capacity of Old Fashioned glasses can vary slightly, but it's likely around 6 to 10 ounces (180 to 300 milliliters).

2 DOUBLE OLD FASHIONED GLASS (DOF)

Just a larger version of your Old Fashioned glass with a capacity typically closer to 15 ounces (450 milliliters). It's often used for drinks with either a lot of liquid, a lot of ice, or both. DOFs are great for tiki drinks if you aren't into or don't have tiki mugs.

3 V-SHAPED MARTINI GLASS

Most see this as the iconic cocktail glass, designed for cocktails served "up" (meaning without ice). The long stem allows you to grip the glass without warming the cocktail with your hand, and the wide mouth is ideal for aromatic cocktails or big garnishes. Recently this glass has fallen out of favor in the cocktail world as its top-heavy design and oversized capacity makes it easy to spill drinks. I never use one, instead opting for a coupe.

4 COUPE

Sometimes called a "Champagne coupe," today this shallow, stemmed, bowl-shaped glass has largely replaced the martini glass for cocktails served up, and is also often utilized for Champagne cocktails. I use a 5.5-ounce (160-milliliter) capacity coupe for most of my sour cocktails, though you can find larger coupes that are ideal for egg-white cocktails or other drinks with more volume.

5 NICK & NORA GLASS

Somewhere between a stemmed wineglass and a coupe is the Nick & Nora, named after *The Thin Man* series characters Nick and Nora Charles, who made frequent use of this drinkware. This glass has a similar capacity to a coupe and can be used interchangeably; it's really just a matter of preference and style. I tend to use it for stirred cocktails served up, like the Manhattan.

6 CHAMPAGNE FLUTE

Whether stemmed or stemless, the Champagne flute is often tapered inward toward the top. This preserves the carbonation by reducing the surface area from which it can escape. The flute is used for Champagne cocktails, like the French 75, as well as other drinks topped with sparkling wine.

7 COLLINS/ HIGHBALL GLASS

This tall glass is ideal for highballs with carbonated ingredients served with ice, such as the Tom Collins or gin and tonic. Technically, a Collins glass is a bit taller and sometimes narrower than a highball glass, but they are used interchangeably.

SWEET, SOUR, BITTER, AND SALTY

ALL COCKTAILS WILL INVOLVE SOME KIND OF FLAVORING BEYOND THE BASE SPIRIT, SO IT'S IMPORTANT TO UNDERSTAND SOME OF THE FUNDAMENTAL FLAVOR PROFILES AND HOW THEY CAN AFFECT THE TASTE AND BALANCE OF A COCKTAIL.

SWEETENERS

Almost every cocktail involves some kind of sweetener. Instead of granulated sugar, syrups are often used because they dissolve faster and allow you to use the same tools for measuring liquids. You should think of simple syrup as your baseline sweetener, with other sweeteners adding more complex flavors and possibly different amounts of sugar by volume. Following are the syrups I use the most to sweeten my cocktails, and in some cases I modify them to achieve the same sweetness as simple syrup (either to make them easier to pour or to seamlessly swap them for simple syrup in existing recipes). Note that with all of the following syrups, you can add fruits or herbs to change up the flavor.

SIMPLE SYRUP

SWEETNESS
50% sugar by weight

INSTRUCTIONS
Combine 1 part sugar (see Note) with 1 part water (by weight) in a saucepan (or roughly equal parts by volume). Bring to a simmer, stirring occasionally, until the syrup is clear. Remove from the heat and let cool. Alternatively, combine 1 part superfine sugar with 1 part water (by weight) in a jar and shake until the sugar is dissolved.

USAGE
Default sweetener in cocktails; most recipes call for simple syrup

STORAGE
Add 1 tablespoon of vodka to the simple syrup and store in the fridge for up to three months.

NOTE
You can use granulated, raw cane, brown, Demerara, or any other sugar for this syrup.

RICH SIMPLE SYRUP

SWEETNESS

66% sugar by weight

INSTRUCTIONS

Combine 2 parts sugar with 1 part water (by weight) in a saucepan. Bring to a simmer, stirring occasionally, until the syrup is clear. Remove from the heat and let cool.

USAGE

Usually as a sweetener for spirit-forward drinks, where you want as little dilution as possible

STORAGE

Add 1 tablespoon of vodka to the syrup and store in the fridge for up to six months.

MAPLE SYRUP

SWEETNESS

67% sugar by weight

INSTRUCTIONS

Add maple syrup directly, then shake or stir in cocktails. Preferably use "Grade A: Dark Color & Robust Taste" syrup.

USAGE

The delicious rich flavor is ideal for pairing with dark spirits, such as bourbon or rye in an Old Fashioned.

AGAVE SYRUP

SWEETNESS

75% sugar by weight

INSTRUCTIONS

Add agave syrup directly, then shake in cocktails or make a simple syrup equivalent by shaking together 50 grams of water with every 100 grams of agave syrup.

USAGE

Goes well with lemon-based cocktails because agave syrup's fast-acting sweetness (due to its high concentration of fructose) complements the fast-acting acidity of lemon.

HONEY SYRUP

SWEETNESS

82% sugar by weight

INSTRUCTIONS

Because honey is too thick to mix directly into cocktails, make a simple syrup equivalent by combining 64 grams of water for every 100 grams of honey (or roughly equal parts by volume) in a saucepan. Bring to a simmer, stirring occasionally, until the honey is dissolved. Remove from the heat and let cool.

USAGE

Most bartenders use a neutral honey like clover, but you can experiment with different varieties.

STORAGE

Add 1 tablespoon of vodka to the honey syrup and store in the fridge for up to one month.

CITRUS JUICES (AND HOW TO DEPLOY THEM IN SOUR COCKTAILS)

While sweeteners are used in almost every cocktail, citrus juice is often only used in shaken cocktails and needs to be balanced with the sugar. So, it's helpful to always think about citrus in relation to the sweetener, which can be difficult as the acidity in citrus varies with ripeness and seasonality.

But if you only take away one thing from this section: use fresh juices. When it comes to making a proper craft cocktail, the juice is worth the squeeze. The following are the most common citrus juices, and I've provided a base template for each one.

LEMON JUICE AND LIME JUICE

These are the most common citrus juices in a sour cocktail. They generally have the same amount of acidity so can be used interchangeably, though lemon tends to pair better with brown spirits like whiskey, and lime with clear spirits like white rum or blanco tequila.

Why is this? One theory is that lemon is composed entirely of citric acid, which is fast acting and fast fading. This paves the way for the polyphenols from wooden barrel–aged spirits that hit the middle of the palate. Lime, on the other hand, is a mix of citric and malic acid, the latter of which has a more delayed impact on your palate.

Here is a standard template for a sour cocktail, but feel free to adjust based on your preferred level of sweetness or acidity in cocktails.

2 ounces (60 ml) spirit of your choice, preferably 80 proof

¾ ounce (22 ml) fresh lemon or lime juice

¾ ounce (22 ml) simple syrup (page 14)

Add all of the ingredients to a shaker tin with ice. Shake and double strain (pour through a Hawthorne strainer over a fine-mesh strainer) into a chilled glass.

GRAPEFRUIT JUICE

I love the bittersweet, refreshing flavor of grapefruit juice with ingredients like Aperol, blanco tequila, or white rum. It has about half the acidity of lemon or lime juice and about six times the sugar, meaning you can't simply substitute grapefruit juice for lemon or lime juice in cocktail recipes. Here's a template you can use instead.

2 ounces (60 ml) spirit of your choice, preferably 100 proof

¾ ounce (22 ml) fresh grapefruit juice

½ ounce (15 ml) fresh lemon or lime juice

½ ounce (15 ml) simple syrup (page 14)

Add all of the ingredients to a shaker tin with ice. Shake and double strain (pour through a Hawthorne strainer over a fine-mesh strainer) into a chilled glass.

ORANGE JUICE

Fresh orange juice can be wonderful in cocktails, especially with rum, whiskey, and gin. But it can be a bit harder to balance because orange juice has a significantly higher sugar-to-acid ratio compared to lemon or lime juice. Here's a template to get you started.

2 ounces (60 ml) spirit of your choice, preferably 100 proof

¾ ounce (22 ml) fresh orange juice

¾ ounce (22 ml) fresh lime or lemon juice

½ ounce (15 ml) simple syrup (page 14)

Add all of the ingredients to a shaker tin with ice. Shake and double strain (pour through a Hawthorne strainer over a fine-mesh strainer) into a chilled glass.

PINEAPPLE JUICE

While technically not a citrus fruit, the sweet, tropical flavor of pineapple makes it one of my favorite juices to use in tequila, mezcal, or rum cocktails. It also creates a wonderful foam when shaken. As with other fruits, the sweetness and acidity levels can vary widely, but here is a template to play with.

2 ounces (60 ml) spirit of your choice, preferably 100 proof

1 ounce (30 ml) fresh pineapple juice

½ ounce (15 ml) fresh lime or lemon juice

½ ounce (15 ml) simple syrup (page 14)

Add all of the ingredients to a shaker tin with ice. Shake and double strain (pour through a Hawthorne strainer over a fine-mesh strainer) into a chilled glass.

BITTERS

Just a few dashes of bitters can add more complexity to your drink by engaging the bitter taste receptors in your palate. I think of bitters as pepper for your cocktail, something to spice it up and make it interesting. They often are made by steeping herbs, roots, bark, or fruit in high-proof alcohol to extract a concentrated flavor. When bitter elements are not involved, the result is called a tincture, and really any flavor can be concentrated into a tincture.

Aromatic bitters, such as Angostura, are the most common category, balancing a variety of botanicals. Citrus bitters, such as orange, are also used in many cocktail recipes, often combined with aromatic bitters. The bitters market has exploded in recent years, so if there's a flavor you'd like to see, it's likely someone has created it at this point.

I recommend grabbing a bottle of Angostura and a variety pack of small bottles of other bitters to taste and experiment with in cocktails.

ADDING SALT
TO COCKTAILS

If bitters are your cocktail's pepper, then salt is . . . the salt. We aren't looking to make your drink salty, but as any baker knows, a pinch of salt can enhance sweet and sour flavors while tempering bitterness. This same concept applies to cocktails and can really brighten them.

Instead of pinching grains of salt, bartenders running around with wet hands prefer to bottle a saline solution (salt water) and add just a drop or two to each cocktail. If you want to see the dramatic effect of salt in cocktails, pour two shots of Campari and add a drop of saline solution to one of them. That shot will be noticeably sweeter and less bitter than the one without. Here is a recipe for a 20% saline solution.

MAKES 5½ TABLESPOONS (80 ML)

0.7 ounces (20 g) kosher salt

5½ tablespoons (80 ml) water

Combine the salt and water in a small jar and shake until the saline solution is clear. Transfer to a dropper dispenser. Add 2 drops of the saline solution to each cocktail before shaking or stirring. Store the saline solution at room temperature for up to three months.

THE VESPER MARTINI
and other martini recipes

RECREATED

James Bond ordered this drink in the novel *Casino Royale* (adapted for the big screen in 2006) in what I would consider to be ultimately doing a disservice to the bartender and to the other card players he suckered into copying his order. But I'm getting ahead of myself. Let's set the scene:

Bond is in a high-stakes poker game at the Casino Royale in Montenegro against the villain-of-the-day Le Chiffre and others, when the bartender comes to the table to offer Bond a drink. Bond instinctively orders a dry martini, but suddenly changes his order to a very specific, nonexistent cocktail. "Three measures of Gordon's gin, one of vodka, half a measure of Kina Lillet. Shake it over ice, and add a thin slice of lemon peel."

All while never breaking eye contact with Le Chiffre. Total power move. Other players at the table are intrigued and jump on board to order the same. The drink is later named after the Bond girl Vesper Lynd. Unfortunately, for all those involved, the Vesper martini is a pretty mediocre cocktail.

Let's start with one important detail: Kina Lillet has not existed since 1986. Lillet Blanc is often used instead, but it's an entirely different aperitif that lacks the bitterness from the quinine in the original.

There are a few products on the market today that can approximate the original Kina Lillet, namely, Cocchi Americano or the wonderful Kina L'Aéro d'Or. You can use either of these in place of the Kina Lillet.

Here are the specs I would use to make a normal-size cocktail, with the ratios that Bond specified:

MAKES 1 DRINK

1½ ounces (45 ml) Gordon's gin

½ ounce (15 ml) vodka

¼ ounce (7 ml) Kina Lillet (use Cocchi Americano or Kina L'Aéro d'Or as substitutes)

1 lemon twist, for garnish

Add the gin, vodka, and Kina to a shaker tin with ice. Shake and double strain (pour through a Hawthorne strainer over a fine-mesh strainer) into a chilled martini glass. Squeeze the lemon twist to express the essential oils over the drink, drop in the twist, and serve.

MAKES 1 DRINK

2 ounces (60 ml) vodka

¼ ounce (7 ml) dry vermouth

Green olive brine, to taste (I add about 3 barspoons)

5 green olives, skewered on a cocktail pick, for garnish

INSPIRED BY IRON MAN

THE DRY, DIRTY VODKA MARTINI

Let's compare Bond's Vesper martini to another big-screen martini order. In the first *Iron Man* movie (2008), the protagonist, Tony Stark, and his assistant, Pepper Potts, share a sexually charged slow dance at a charity ball, as well as a near-kiss experience after they step outside to get some air. So how do you ease the tension after that? How about a bucket of booze disguised as a cocktail? Tony is happy to oblige her request for a very dry vodka martini with olives. Lots of olives.

As we're learning in the following pages, "dry" means not sweet, implying a higher ratio of spirit (in this case, vodka) to vermouth. "Extra dry" takes that even further, suggesting just a hint of vermouth. So yeah, a glass of vodka. Throw in some olive brine for some flavor (and to make it "dirty").

Add the vodka, vermouth, and olive brine to a mixing glass with ice and stir for about 45 seconds. Double strain (pour through a Hawthorne strainer over a fine-mesh strainer) into a chilled Nick & Nora glass and garnish with the olives.

A QUICK PRIMER ON THE MARTINI

ORDERING A MARTINI IS A LOT LIKE ORDERING A COFFEE. YOUR TALL, HALF-CAF, NONFAT LATTE WITH A CARAMEL DRIZZLE IS COMPARABLE TO YOUR VODKA MARTINI, EXTRA DRY, A BIT DIRTY WITH FIVE OLIVES, AND A LEMON TWIST. BEFORE I DIVE INTO THE RECIPES FOR THIS ICONIC COCKTAIL AND ITS SPINOFFS, LET'S FIRST DISCUSS THE BASIC COMPONENTS AND LANGUAGE OF THE MARTINI ORDER.

THE LANGUAGE OF THE MARTINI

BASE SPIRIT
Vodka or gin are the standard choices. Gin will often have more character and variation depending on which gin you choose (Hendrick's, for example, will be quite distinct from, say, Tanqueray, which is a London dry gin). Vodka will showcase the other ingredients in the drink more prominently since it's a neutral spirit.

MODIFIER
Often a dry vermouth, which is an aromatized and fortified wine. This gives the drink some body and sweetness, and makes it a proper cocktail instead of just a bucket of alcohol.

DRY

"Dry" literally means "not sweet." So, here's the confusing part—if you order a "dry martini," you are actually requesting less dry vermouth (since dry vermouth is still a bit sweet). By specifying how dry you want your martini, you're guiding the bartender about your preferred ratio of spirit-to-vermouth. You'll see some examples later in this section.

DIRTY

"Dirty" refers to the addition of green olive brine. If you order your martini dirty or extra dirty, you're asking for a few barspoons of olive brine to be mixed into the cocktail, which gives it a savory flavor.

GARNISH

Don't underestimate the impact of the garnish on the flavor. Expressing the essential oils from a lemon twist will brighten up the drink and even evolve it over time. Other common garnishes include:

GREEN OLIVES

(often served in odd numbers in a dirty martini)

PICKLED COCKTAIL ONIONS

(found in the martini variation called "The Gibson").

GLASSWARE

Martinis are almost exclusively served "up" (in a stemmed glass without ice). I find the traditional V-shaped martini glass to be a terrible vessel—it's too big and top heavy, forcing you to hold the V part to stabilize the glass and thus warming the drink with your hand. I'd recommend a coupe or Nick & Nora glass instead. Oh, and always chill your glass in the freezer ahead of time, or with ice water while you prepare the drink.

If that wasn't enough, there is also the infamous question of whether to shake or stir a martini. It's a heated debate that deserves its own discussion later on, and we can largely thank James Bond for adding to that confusion (see Shaken or Stirred?, page 30).

CLASSIC GIN MARTINI

This is the cocktail to showcase the nuances of the botanicals in gin. I recommend starting with a London dry gin and then experiment from there with other styles of gin. Here is my go-to recipe for this classic, and do not skip the lemon twist!

Add the gin, vermouth, and bitters to a mixing glass with ice. Stir and strain into a chilled coupe. Squeeze the lemon twist to express the essential oils over the drink, drop in the twist, and serve.

RELATED

MAKES 1 DRINK

2 ounces (60 ml) London dry gin

1 ounce (30 ml) dry vermouth

1 dash orange bitters

1 lemon twist, for garnish

RELATED

CORPSE REVIVER #2

MAKES 1 DRINK

¾ ounce (22 ml) London dry gin

¾ ounce (22 ml) Cointreau

¾ ounce (22 ml) Cocchi Americano

¾ ounce (22 ml) fresh lemon juice

Absinthe, for spraying or rinsing the glass

1 lemon twist, for garnish

If you tried your hand at the Vesper Martini (page 21), you've likely invested in a bottle of Cocchi Americano or something similar to replicate the flavor of the discontinued Kina Lillet. Here's a drink that puts it to good use and has the added bonus of being an equal parts cocktail. This is, by far, the most popular of the Corpse Reviver cocktails, first popularized in *The Savoy Cocktail Book* in 1930.

Add the gin, Cointreau, Cocchi, and lemon juice to a shaker tin with ice and shake for 15 seconds. Spray or rinse a chilled coupe with absinthe. Double strain (pour through a Hawthorne strainer over a fine-mesh strainer) into the prepared glass. Squeeze the lemon twist to express the essential oils over the drink, drop in the twist, and serve.

THE MARTINEZ

The history of this drink is a bit murky (as with most classic cocktails), and some claim it actually predated the martini. Regardless, it's one of my favorites that swaps the dry vermouth for sweet vermouth and adds a few more bells and whistles. I like to use Old Tom gin, which is a sweeter, less juniper-forward style gin than London dry gin. The ratio of gin to sweet vermouth varies across different classic recipe books, but this is my preferred recipe.

Add the gin, vermouth, maraschino liqueur, and both bitters to a mixing glass. Stir with ice for about 45 seconds. Strain into a chilled Nick & Nora glass. Squeeze the lemon twist to express the essential oils over the drink, drop in the twist, and serve.

MAKES 1 DRINK

2 ounces (60 ml) Old Tom gin

1 ounce (30 ml) sweet vermouth

1 barspoon (5 ml) maraschino liqueur

1 dash Angostura bitters

1 dash orange bitters

1 lemon twist, for garnish

SHAKEN OR STIRRED?
THE SCIENCE OF DILUTION

One of the top comments I get on my YouTube videos relates to shaking versus stirring. I'm going to nerd out a bit on the science of dilution, but if your attention span is as short as mine, here are the most important takeaways:

SHAKING AND STIRRING serve three primary purposes:

- mix the ingredients
- chill the drink
- add dilution from the resulting melted ice

Shaking has the added purpose of aerating the drink for texture.

A SIMPLE RULE OF THUMB is to shake when citrus juice is involved. Shaken cocktail recipes are designed to be served colder and with more dilution.

SHAKING A SPIRIT-FORWARD COCKTAIL (like a martini or Manhattan) isn't objectively wrong, but it will be colder and more diluted and aerated. Personal preference always trumps the cocktail "rules," so make the drink you or your guest prefers.

HOW TO SHAKE A COCKTAIL

First, let's cover the basic steps of shaking any cocktail:

1. Grab your favorite shaker tin. I strongly prefer a Boston shaker, which consists of two tins (or one tin and one pint glass) vs. a cobbler shaker, but either works.

2. Add your liquid ingredients to the smaller tin. Best practice is to start with the cheaper ingredients in case you mess up, but this is more relevant for professional bartenders.

3. Add four ice cubes straight from the freezer.

4. Combine the two tins (if using a Boston shaker) and create a tight seal; the smaller tin (or pint glass) should be at an angle so that part of it rests against the rim of the larger tin (see photo on page 31).

5. Shake with a bit of vim and vigor for 12 to 15 seconds.

> To easily separate the shaker tins after shaking a cocktail, use your wrist to hit the bottom tin just outside where it makes contact with the top tin.

6. Press a Hawthorne strainer against the larger tin to hold back the chunks of ice and any other solid ingredients and pour the drink through a fine-mesh strainer into your chilled glass. The fine-mesh strainer will catch the small ice chips and any citrus pulp. This is called "double straining."

7. Garnish and serve.

COMMON QUESTIONS ABOUT SHAKING

WHAT HAPPENS IF I SHAKE A COCKTAIL WITHOUT CITRUS?

The ghost of Jerry Thomas appears and gives you one bartender demerit. Spirit-forward cocktails, like the martini, were designed to be stirred, but honestly that doesn't mean you can't shake it. In fact, many prefer it that way. It will be a colder drink (great), but a more diluted drink. If your martini is extra dry and mostly booze, dilution may be your friend. Oh, and if you shook with gin, you won't "bruise" it, as the common misconception goes.

WHY SHAKE WITH FOUR ICE CUBES FOR 12 TO 15 SECONDS?

Thanks to some detailed shaking/stirring experiments from food and drink "mad scientist" Dave Arnold, we learned that shaking a drink for longer than 15 seconds will not result in a meaningfully colder drink, as it will have already reached equilibrium temperature and dilution. When it comes to dilution, the amount and size of ice is less important, as long as there is not much surface water on the ice that can overdilute without chilling the cocktail. I use four 1.25-inch square ice cubes, as you simply need to use "enough" ice to sufficiently chill and dilute the drink. You could use five cubes with similar results.

HOW TO STIR A COCKTAIL

Let's cover the basic steps of stirring a cocktail:

1. Grab something to mix it in. This could be a cocktail mixing glass, but any cylindrical glass will do. In a pinch, just use a pint glass.

2. Stir with a proper barspoon. The long stem allows for the smooth stirring motion that you will struggle to replicate with your standard dining spoon.

3. Build your cocktail ingredients in the mixing glass, then add four ice cubes. Adding the ice last is an easy way to avoid unnecessary dilution (though some bartenders prefer to chill the mixing glass with ice, then dump any excess water).

4. Now comes the stir—this technique takes a little bit of practice. Pinch the stem of the barspoon with your thumb and index finger, then below that, let the stem rest between your ring and middle fingers. Place the spoon against the inside of the glass. You'll want the bowl of the spoon facing inward.

5. Holding the mixing glass with your free hand, press the barspoon against the edge of the glass and stir using a push/pull motion with the spoon. It might feel awkward at first, but just practice with ice water for 5 to 10 minutes and you'll get it down.

> **TO STIR A COCKTAIL:** Pinch the stem of the barspoon with your thumb and index finger, let the stem rest between your ring and middle fingers, and stir using a push/pull motion with the spoon against the wall of the mixing glass.

COMMON QUESTIONS ABOUT STIRRING

DOES THE SIZE OF ICE MATTER?

When it comes to stirring, yes it does have a fairly large impact. Unlike shaking, we are not going to cool to an equilibrium temperature, and so I find the ideal temperature and dilution to come from 45 seconds of stirring with four 1.25-inch square ice cubes. Conveniently, this is the same amount of ice I use for shaking.

DO I REALLY NEED TO STIR FOR 45 SECONDS?

You can cut this time down by using smaller bits of ice, which will cool and dilute faster. There's a nuance here, though: small ice that's already been crushed will actually hold a nontrivial amount of water on the surface, so introducing that into the mixing glass will add some dilution without cooling. This is why you often see bartenders take a large cube of ice and crack it with the back of the bar spoon into the glass, yielding smaller ice with no surface water, and thus shorter stirring time. While that technique works for a bar, it can get a bit messy at home, so I prefer to just stir the 45 seconds with the 1.25-inch ice cubes.

WON'T THE ICE COOL THE DRINK FASTER IF MY FREEZER IS SET TO A LOWER TEMPERATURE?

This is one of those areas that might seem counterintuitive, but ice temperature actually doesn't have a meaningful effect on the process at all. This is largely due to the fact that once you pull it from the freezer, ice will reach 32°F (0°C) very quickly, likely before you begin the mixing process. Ice is a great conductor of heat, so it doesn't take a lot of energy to heat it.

BART'S MANHATTAN

and other manhattan recipes

Back in 1991, a young Cocktail Chemist may have witnessed his very first cocktail recipe on TV. Between the ages of seven and twelve, my weekday evenings consisted of at least two episodes of *The Simpsons*, in what is now considered the golden era of the series. Season three featured an episode titled "Bart the Murderer," where Bart finds himself behind the stick at the Legitimate Businessman's Social Club, a mob bar owned by Fat Tony and the mafia. Bart's signature drink is the Manhattan, which he recreates from a dusty recipe on the wall.

Add the bourbon, vermouth, and bitters to a shaker tin with ice. Shake and strain into a chilled martini glass. Drop in the cherry and serve.

RECREATED

MAKES 1 DRINK

1½ ounces (45 ml) bourbon or rye

½ ounce (15 ml) sweet vermouth

1 dash Angostura bitters

1 maraschino cherry, for garnish

RELATED

MAKES 1 DRINK

---

2 ounces (60 ml) rye

1 ounce (30 ml) sweet vermouth (I like to use Carpano Antica)

2 dashes Angostura bitters

1 maraschino cherry (I typically use Luxardo brand), for garnish

CLASSIC MANHATTAN

With quality ingredients, there's nothing terribly wrong with Bart's version of this classic cocktail. I have a few quibbles, though: He shakes when you really should stir the drink (refer to my discussion of shaking vs. stirring and the science of dilution on page 30), and he uses those bright red cherries that are often rubbery and overly sweet. His ingredient ratios are also a bit different from what you'd typically see today in a Manhattan, but let's explore the history a bit for this one. Again, the true origin story is murky, as is often the case with these iconic cocktails. Most believe the Manhattan was created in New York City around 1880 and was one of the first cocktails to utilize sweet vermouth to soften the harshness of the whiskey. The drink was traditionally made with rye, which was a popular spirit in the nineteenth century.

There are many ways to build this cocktail, but my preferred specs are 2-1-2, which is a mnemonic for 2 ounces of whiskey, 1 ounce of vermouth, and 2 dashes of bitters. It also happens to be one of the area codes for the borough of Manhattan. Instead of garnishing with the bright red, artificially flavored cherries that Bart uses, I usually upgrade to a higher quality brand like Luxardo.

Add the rye, vermouth, and bitters to a mixing glass with ice. Stir until chilled and strain into a chilled Nick & Nora glass. Drop in the cherry and serve.

MAKES 1 DRINK

2 ounces (60 ml) bourbon

1 ounce (30 ml) Averna amaro

1 dash Angostura bitters

1 dash orange bitters

1 maraschino cherry
(I typically use Luxardo brand), for garnish

BLACK MANHATTAN

The Black Manhattan is probably my favorite of the Manhattan "cousins." This riff swaps out the sweet vermouth for Averna amaro, which is a nineteenth-century herbal elixir originating from Italy and, like many amari, the recipe is a secret. With a mix of herbs, bark, citrus peel, berries, and roots creating a more bittersweet flavor, Averna is certainly much more complex than most sweet vermouths I've tried.

It's believed that the Black Manhattan was created at Bourbon & Branch in San Francisco, and I would go so far as to call it a modern classic. The drink is dark, rich, and full-bodied—any fan of a Manhattan should add this to their cocktail arsenal. I find that bourbon, which has a sweeter profile than rye, complements the Averna better in this recipe.

Add the bourbon, amaro, and both bitters to a mixing glass with ice. Stir until chilled and strain into a chilled Nick & Nora glass. Drop in the cherry and serve.

PERFECT MANHATTAN

MAKES 1 DRINK

2 ounces (60 ml) rye or bourbon

½ ounce (15 ml) sweet vermouth

½ ounce (15 ml) dry vermouth

2 dashes Angostura bitters

1 lemon twist, for garnish

Okay, so you're probably here expecting me to give you the perfect recipe for a Manhattan, implying that I intentionally listed an inferior recipe at the beginning of this section. How dare you. But understandable.

In fact, "Perfect Manhattan" does not refer to a flawless version of the cocktail, it's the name of the cocktail, defined by splitting the sweet vermouth into equal parts sweet and dry vermouth. "Dry" means "not sweet," so if you find Manhattans to be too sweet, this might be the recipe you've been waiting for.

I also recommend swapping the maraschino cherry garnish for a lemon twist if you've got a palate that prefers drier flavors.

Add the rye, both vermouths, and the bitters to a mixing glass with ice. Stir until chilled and strain into a chilled Nick & Nora glass. Squeeze the lemon twist to express the essential oils over the drink, drop in the twist, and serve.

THE DUDE'S WHITE RUSSIAN

and other coffee liqueur cocktails

In 1998, *The Big Lebowski* by the Coen brothers hit the big screens. While it was far from a box office hit, it's since grown into a very quotable cult classic. The movie also helped revive the popularity of one of the most iconic coffee liqueur cocktails: the White Russian.

The film's protagonist, Jeffrey "The Dude" Lebowski, is a man of simple pleasures: bowling, rugs that tie rooms together, and White Russians.

The Dude imbibes. In fact, he imbibes nine White Russians throughout the movie, each made with Kahlúa coffee liqueur, Smirnoff vodka, and whatever milk product he has lying around the bar (ranging from half-and-half to powdered creamer). The idea of a measured recipe that involves any kind of precision is really against all that The Dude stands for, but here are the rough specs you're going for.

Fill a rocks glass with ice. Add all the ingredients and stir with your finger. Wipe that finger on your bathrobe. Imbibe.

RECREATED

MAKES 1 DRINK

1½ ounces (45 ml) vodka (ideally something Russian)

1 ounce (30 ml) coffee liqueur

1 ounce (30 ml) half-and-half

Many White Russian recipes call for heavy cream instead of half-and-half, which definitely works. But if you're looking to put away a few of these in one night, you may opt for the lighter half-and-half. But that's just, like, my opinion, man.

IMPROVED WHITE RUSSIAN

MAKES 1 DRINK

1½ ounces (45 ml) vodka (ideally something Russian)

1½ ounces (45 ml) coffee liqueur (see page 45 for a homemade version)

1½ ounces (45 ml) Toasted Cream (recipe follows)

Often when I recreate drinks from pop culture, I follow them with my own take on the drink using some more advanced techniques. Warning: This variation involves several steps and some fancy equipment, making it decidedly "un-Dude." But the result is truly an elevated White Russian if you're willing to put in a bit of work.

The secret ingredient here is "toasted cream" instead of regular cream or half-and-half, a technique introduced by Sohla El-Waylly for *Serious Eats* in 2018. What the hell is toasted cream, exactly? In the same way that heating butter turns it into "brown butter," slow and low heating of cream will result in a light brown, nutty-flavored cream that's the perfect complement to coffee. This works because of what's called the Maillard reaction, a complex array of chemical reactions that occur when sugars and proteins are broken down in the dairy. There's also a bit of caramelization at play here. By using an immersion circulator (aka cooking it sous vide), you can gently heat the cream in a temperature-controlled water bath and get full control over the cooking process.

Adding a bit of baking soda can speed up the Maillard reaction, as well. Here are the specs for making a White Russian with sous-vide toasted cream, with an option to toast the cream in a pressure cooker to speed up the process.

Add the vodka, liqueur, and toasted cream to a shaker tin with ice. Shake for 10 seconds. Double strain (pour through a Hawthorne strainer over a fine-mesh strainer) into a double Old Fashioned glass over a large ice cube (preferably one that's clear; see Clear Ice on page 54) and serve.

Toasted Cream

MAKES 16 OUNCES (473 ML)

1 pint (473 ml) heavy cream

¼ teaspoon (2 g) baking soda

1. Whisk the cream and baking soda together in a liquid measuring cup. Pour into a gallon-size zip-top plastic bag or vacuum-sealable bag, remove the air, and seal.

2. Fill a tall, large pot or other heatproof container with water. Attach or stand an immersion circulator in it, set it to 180°F (82°C), then drop in the bag. If the bag isn't fully submerged in the water, weigh it down with an inverted vegetable steamer basket. Let cook for 24 hours.

3. Remove the bag from the water. Open or snip a corner from the bag and strain the toasted cream through a fine-mesh sieve set over a jar; discard the solids. Cover and refrigerate until the toasted cream is chilled. You can keep the toasted cream in an airtight container in the fridge for up to seven days.

PRESSURE COOKER VARIATION: Alternatively, you can use a pressure cooker and mason jars for a faster result. Divide the cream and baking soda mixture between two 12-ounce mason jars; screw the lids on very loosely so the jars don't break. Place the steamer rack in the pressure cooker, add about an inch of water, and put the jars on top of the rack. Cook at full pressure for 2 hours, then let the pressure release naturally. Strain and refrigerate the toasted cream, following the sous-vide directions.

Congratulations, you've now got toasted cream. Your hipster score went up by ten points. While this works great in a White Russian, it's also a wonderfully nutty enhancement to your morning coffee.

HOMEMADE COFFEE LIQUEUR

RELATED

Coffee liqueur is one of those products that's pretty easy to replicate at home, and if you're like me, you'll appreciate that you can make something that's less sweet than many of the popular brands. Not only can you dial down that sweetness, you can take advantage of freshly ground coffee to make a brighter liqueur.

MAKES 28 OUNCES (830 ML)

¼ cup (20 g) ground espresso beans

1¼ cups (300 ml), plus 1 cup (240 ml) water

1 cup (200 g) turbinado sugar

2 cups (½ liter) dark rum

1 teaspoon (5 ml) pure vanilla extract

1. Combine the ground espresso beans with 1¼ cups (300 ml) water in a 1-pint mason jar. Cover, gently shake to combine, then refrigerate for 12 hours.

2. Combine the sugar with 1 cup (240 ml) water in a small saucepan. Bring to a simmer over low heat, stirring to dissolve the sugar. Remove from the heat and let cool.

3. Strain the cold brew coffee through a coffee filter–lined sieve set over a large jar. Add the cooled sugar syrup, rum, and vanilla. Cover, shake, and store in the fridge, where it will stay bright and flavorful for up to two months.

RELATED

ESPRESSO MARTINI

MAKES 1 DRINK

1½ ounces (45 ml) vodka

1½ ounces (45 ml) fresh brewed hot espresso

1 ounce (30 ml) coffee liqueur (see page 45 for a homemade version)

¼ ounce (7 ml) simple syrup (page 14)

Espresso beans, for garnish

The espresso martini is a cocktail that comes with a tagline: the drink that will wake you up and f*ck you up. But, made correctly, this can be a complex and delicious drink with an incredible texture and just the right amount of sweetness. The key to a great espresso martini is, of course, a well-pulled shot of espresso (don't even think about calling it "expresso") but I'll leave that technique to the coffee nerds.

Here are the standard specs, but note that the amount of simple syrup is highly dependent on the type of coffee liqueur you use and your preferred sweetness. Start with these measurements and adjust to your palate.

Add the vodka, espresso, coffee liqueur, and simple syrup to a shaker tin with ice. Shake for 15 seconds. Double strain (pour through a Hawthorne strainer over a fine-mesh strainer) into a chilled martini glass or coupe. Garnish with the espresso beans and serve.

Using freshly pulled espresso for an espresso martini will result in a delightful foam on top.

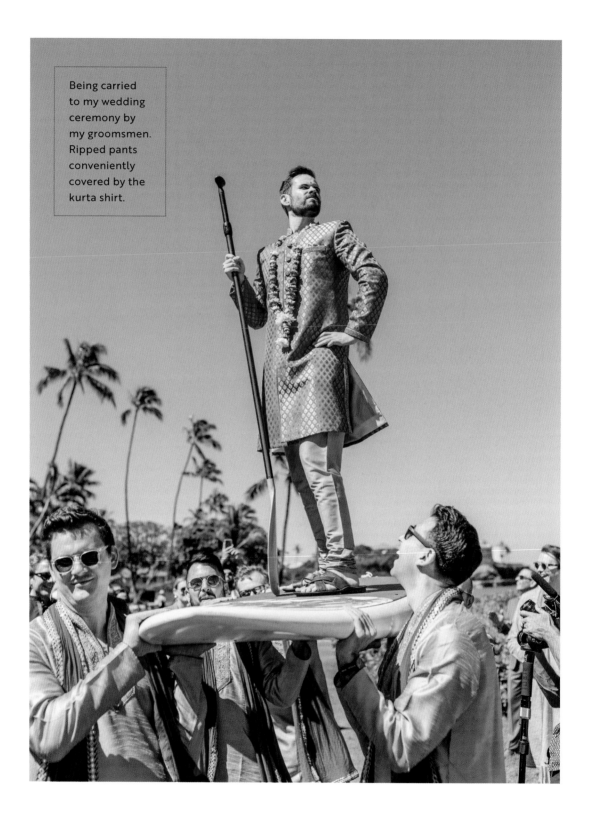

Being carried to my wedding ceremony by my groomsmen. Ripped pants conveniently covered by the kurta shirt.

COAST-TO-COAST

My partner, Rishita, and I got married in Maui in 2018. She's of Indian descent and there was never any doubt we wanted an epic four-day traditional Indian wedding. (Though for my groom's entrance, we swapped the customary horse for a surfboard, and I may have ripped my pants upon boarding it.) As you can imagine, expectations were high for the reception cocktails, and the hotel mai tais weren't going to cut it. So, I designed a trio of "his," "her," and "us" cocktails that told a bit of a story, including this original creation that I called the "Coast-to-Coast."

The name reflects my bicoastal roots, growing up in Seattle then spending my twenties in New York City, where I met my partner. I tried to capture that by combining Seattle's coffee obsession with a Manhattan cocktail, and it turned out awesome.

Add the rye, vermouth, coffee liqueur, and both bitters to a mixing glass with ice. Stir for about 45 seconds. Strain into a chilled Nick & Nora glass and serve.

RELATED

MAKES 1 DRINK

---

2 ounces (60 ml) rye

½ ounce (15 ml) sweet vermouth

½ ounce (15 ml) coffee liqueur (see page 45 for a homemade version)

1 dash chocolate bitters

1 dash orange bitters

DON DRAPER'S OLD FASHIONED

and other old fashioned recipes

RECREATED

MAKES 1 DRINK

1 sugar cube

3 dashes Angostura bitters

1½ ounces (45 ml) rye

1 ounce (30 ml) chilled soda water

1 half orange wheel, for garnish

The 1960s marked the beginning of the "dark ages" of cocktails in American history (generally considered to be between the 1960s and 1990s). We started to see some bizarre cocktail inventions with high marketing budgets and dubious backstories, like the Harvey Wallbanger (page 111), which had one of the strangest ad campaigns with a tweaked out, sandal-clad surfer mascot.

That ad would never fly with Don Draper. The protagonist of the TV show *Mad Men* epitomized the Madison Avenue ad executive, who paired his creative ideas with a few fingers of rye at lunch and a few other vices on the side. The man loved his Old Fashioneds, and the show was credited with helping to bring this classic cocktail back into popularity after *Mad Men* debuted in 2007.

In season three, we actually get to see Don jump behind the bar and make one of these from scratch using the following specs.

1. Add the sugar cube to a rocks glass and shake the bitters over the cube. Muddle them together into a paste.

2. Add the rye to a pint glass with ice, top with the soda water, and give it a brief stir to mix it together. Pour into the rocks glass, ice and all. Garnish with the orange and serve.

CLASSIC OLD FASHIONED

MAKES 1 DRINK

2 ounces (60 ml) rye

2 dashes Angostura bitters

¼ ounce (7 ml) simple syrup (page 14)

1 lemon twist, for garnish

I'm not one to dive deep into cocktail history, as the origin stories are often dubious and rarely satisfying, but, as one of the OG American cocktails, the Old Fashioned deserves a bit of context. Here are some interesting nuggets:

- The original name for the Old Fashioned was the "Whiskey Cocktail," based on the technical definition of a cocktail that first appeared in 1806: "a drink containing a spirit, sugar, water, and bitters."

- The Whiskey Cocktail was first mentioned in the *Bartender's Guide* by Jerry Thomas in 1862, and around that time it was even made in large batches and sold as provisions to the Union Army in the Civil War. During these early years, the drink was regarded as a "matutinal cocktail," meaning you drank it before breakfast.

- In the 1870s, bartenders began making the "improved" Whiskey Cocktail by adding other ingredients, such as absinthe, Curaçao, maraschino cherries, or all three.

- Yet in the late 1870s and early 1880s, principled drinkers decided that these "improved" cocktails were in fact desecrations of the originals, calling for a return to the "old-fashioned" recipes. Hence, the Old Fashioned we know of was given its new name.

Okay, enough history; how should we make this drink? There are a few big choices to make here: Sugar cube or sugar syrup? Rye or bourbon? Lemon twist or orange twist? For the classic version, I go with simple syrup instead of a sugar cube to better incorporate the sugar into the drink (maple syrup also works well here). I like rye for the base because it tends to be a bit spicier than bourbon. And for the garnish, I prefer a lemon twist, as it makes the drink a bit brighter.

Add the rye, bitters, and simple syrup to a mixing glass with ice and stir for about 45 seconds. Strain into a rocks glass over a large ice cube (preferably one that's clear; see Clear Ice on page 54). Squeeze the lemon twist to express the essential oils over the drink, drop in the twist, and serve.

By far the most popular video on my YouTube channel is about making perfectly clear ice at home. People seem to love clear ice, and there's a whole industry around creating large blocks of transparent ice using a Clinebell machine, carving them up with a band saw, and delivering them to craft cocktail bars.

But there are a lot of misconceptions about clear ice, both on how to make it and the benefits it provides. First, let's dispel the biggest misconception that distilled, filtered, or boiled water on its own will freeze into perfectly clear ice. While this isn't true, it can improve the clarity of the ice if your tap water isn't great.

Another common misconception is that clear ice will stay colder and dissolve more slowly because the lack of trapped gases reduces the surface area or makes it more "dense." Plenty of experiments show that this effect is minimal to the point of being imperceptible to the average drinker.

Where does ice cloudiness come from? The three main sources of cloudiness are from dissolved solids, dissolved gasses, and compression that occurs at the end of the freezing process. So, a technique to remove (or isolate) this cloudiness is required to get to the clear stuff.

Enter: "directional freezing." This technique, first demonstrated in 2009 by Camper English of the *Alcademics* blog, is by far the easiest and most economical method of achieving perfectly clear ice at home. In short, by forcing the ice to freeze from the top to the bottom of your vessel (as opposed to outside in with a conventional ice tray), we are able to separate the cloudiness from the clarity.

There are a variety of specialty products on the market that can make this easier for the home bartender, but they are often expensive. I use a simple, inexpensive method for directional freezing, which requires removing the lid from a 5-quart cooler. By removing the top of an otherwise insulated container, you're forcing the ice to freeze from the top down. And if you remove the cooler from the freezer after about 18 hours, the top half of the water will freeze clear while the bottom half remains unfrozen. This simplifies the process so you won't have to chop off any cloudy ice that forms at the bottom.

**5 quarts tap water (use filtered or
distilled water if your tap water is hard
with dissolved solids)**

SPECIAL EQUIPMENT
5-quart cooler, with the lid removed

Mallet or hammer

Serrated knife

1. Fill the cooler with the water and
   place it, uncovered, in the freezer
   until the top half of the water freezes
   clear but the bottom hasn't yet
   frozen, about 18 hours.

2. Remove the cooler from the freezer,
   let sit for 10 minutes, then invert the
   cooler onto a large cutting board in
   the sink and remove the ice block
   (you may have to run warm water
   on the sides or press in the bottom
   of the cooler to help release the ice
   block).

3. The ice block will have a pocket
   of water in an ice shell. Have fun
   smashing the shell to drain the water.
   Use a mallet or hammer to knock
   away jagged edges, then run warm
   water over those edges to smooth out
   the ice block. Using a serrated knife,
   score the surface of the block into
   your desired shapes, such as large
   cubes or sticks. Rest the serrated
   knife along a scored line, then use the
   mallet or hammer to gently tap the
   back of the knife against the ice to
   make clean cuts. Repeat as necessary.
   Freeze the cut ice in a freezer bag
   until ready to use.

IMPORTANT: When removing your clear ice from the
freezer, let it temper (sit at room temperature) for at
least 5 minutes before using, otherwise it might crack
when you pour your cocktail over it—which ruins the
whole point of clear ice. The ice will not lose clarity in
the freezer but may form some frost on the outside.
This will disappear when it comes into contact with
your drink.

After about 18 hours in the freezer, a large clear ice block will have formed
in the cooler and the cloudy section of ice will not yet have formed.

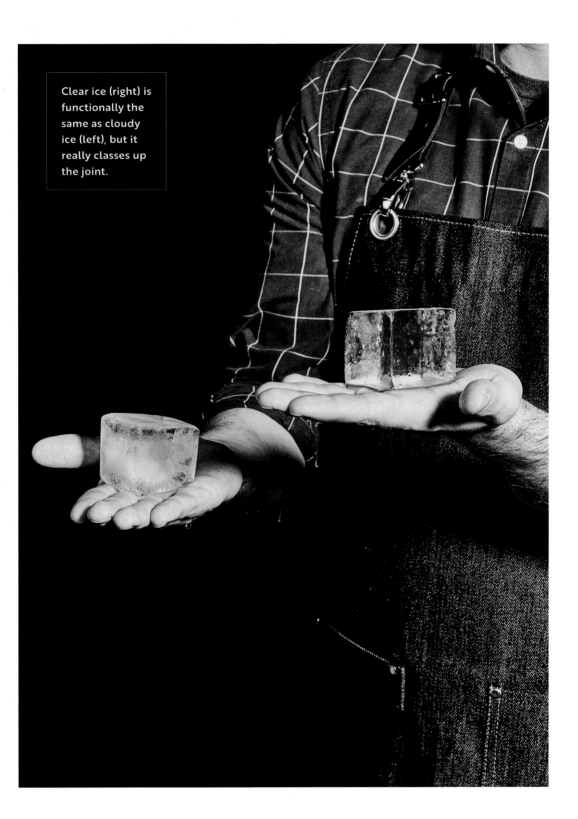

Clear ice (right) is functionally the same as cloudy ice (left), but it really classes up the joint.

WISCONSIN BRANDY OLD FASHIONED

This is probably the most controversial recipe in this book. Why? Because Wisconsin lays claim to a drink that bears the Old Fashioned moniker but includes unconventional ingredients, like 7UP or sour mix. After some deep research on this drink, including consulting with actual Wisconsin bartenders (shout-out to Brian Bartels of the Settle Down Tavern in Madison), I've concluded that the recipe is more of a template, served however the guest prefers, and I like that lack of fussiness around cocktails.

At first glance, this drink is quite similar to a traditional Old Fashioned, just swapping bourbon for brandy. The story goes that German immigrants took a liking to California brandy (specifically the Korbel brand) when they tried it at the 1893 Chicago World's Fair, and they started making classic cocktails with Korbel. These days, Wisconsinites reportedly buy half of Korbel's entire production of brandy.

Again, this drink has become more of a template that can be tailored to personal preference. When you order it in a Wisco bar, you'll typically get asked if you want it "sweet, sour, or press?" A request for "sweet" means adding 7UP, "sour" means adding sour mix or Squirt, and "press" means adding half 7UP and half soda water.

RELATED

MAKES 1 DRINK

1 or 2 maraschino cherries, plus 1 more for garnish

1 half orange wheel, plus 1 more for garnish

1 sugar cube

3 dashes Angostura bitters

2 ounces (60 ml) Korbel brandy

Splash of chilled 7UP, sour mix or Squirt, or a combination of 7UP and soda water

---

Add the cherries, orange wheel, sugar cube, and bitters to a rocks glass. Muddle to extract the juices until the fruits give up most of their liquid and dissolve the sugar cube. Add cracked ice and the brandy and stir. Add the 7UP for "sweet," sour mix or Squirt for "sour," or half 7UP/half soda water for "press." Garnish with the remaining cherry and half orange wheel skewered on a cocktail pick. Enjoy with cheese curds during your Friday night fish fry.

OAXACA OLD FASHIONED

MAKES 1 DRINK

1½ ounces (45 ml) reposado tequila

½ ounce (15 ml) mezcal

2 dashes Angostura bitters

1 barspoon (5 ml) agave syrup

1 orange twist, for garnish

When I lived in the East Village of Manhattan back in my twenties, East 6th Street had some iconic bars that introduced a young Nick to the craft cocktail scene, including Death & Co and the agave-focused Mayahuel. Phil Ward was a founding bartender of both, and he helped bring tequila- and mezcal-forward cocktails and an appreciation for the quality of those spirits into the mainstream. One of those drinks is the legendary Oaxaca Old Fashioned, a brilliant way to enjoy high-quality tequila and mezcal in a spirit-forward cocktail. This drink is typically served with a flamed orange twist, which ignites the fragrant limonene oils held in the peel. While some claim this "caramelizes" the oils, there is no sugar being heated here. The effect is just for show.

Add a large ice cube (preferably one that's clear; see Clear Ice on page 54) to a rocks glass. Add the mezcal, bitters, and agave syrup and stir to chill. Light a match and hold it in one hand, then use your other hand to squeeze the orange twist and express the essential oils over the flame into the drink (see Flaming a Citrus Peel on page 174). Drop in the orange twist and serve.

GREEN RUSSIAN

and other clarified milk punches

The basic pitch for the TV show *Archer* supposedly went something like this: What if James Bond was played by Charlie Sheen as Charlie Sheen? Sterling Archer is that charming, chauvinistic spy who also has a penchant for creative cocktails. I've done several *Archer*-inspired cocktails on my YouTube channel and some have been delicious, others terrible. The original Green Russian falls into the latter category. In the first episode of season two, we see the spy agency's HR director Pam "invent" this drink without much context except that she seems to have a bottle of absinthe and a jug of milk lying around.

While an exact recipe for Pam's Green Russian wasn't specified in the show, a little detective work (asking a writer on the show) gets us pretty close. But let me be clear: Don't make this drink unless you really like your absinthe. The real gold is in the Improved Green Russian (page 64), one of the best cocktails I've created.

You still want the original recipe? Okay, fine. Here it is, but don't say I didn't warn you.

Add the absinthe, vodka, and milk to a rocks glass with ice and stir. Pour contents of glass down the drain (recommended).

RECREATED

MAKES 1 DRINK

1 ounce (30 ml) green absinthe

1 ounce (30 ml) vodka (ideally something Russian)

2 ounces (60 ml) whole milk

IMPROVED GREEN RUSSIAN

**MAKES ABOUT FIVE
5-OUNCE (150-ML)
SERVINGS**

---

1 cup (235 ml) cold
whole milk

2 cups (470 ml) brewed
green tea, chilled
or cooled to room
temperature

⅔ cup (150 ml) Green
Chartreuse

⅔ cup (150 ml) vodka
(ideally something
Russian)

⅓ cup (75 ml) fresh lime
juice

⅓ cup (70 g) sugar

When trying to come up with a way to salvage the Green Russian from *Archer* (page 63), I was looking for a way to incorporate something green into the dairy and vodka elements of a White Russian cocktail. Fans of my channel will know all too well that my favorite green bottle is not absinthe, but Green Chartreuse, a wonderfully complex herbal liqueur created by monks of the Chartreuse region of France.

But instead of just combining all these ingredients together, I decided to turn them into a clarified milk punch. This is a fascinating technique that dates back to the eighteenth century and yields an incredibly rich and shelf-stable batched cocktail. Keep reading for more details on the science behind this technique and some additional recipes.

---

1. Add the milk to a large nonreactive bowl and set aside.

2. Combine the remaining ingredients in a large pitcher or vessel and stir together until the sugar dissolves. Slowly pour into the milk and gently stir until it curdles. Strain through a coffee filter into a large bowl (this could take a couple hours) and discard the filter.

3. Funnel the clarified milk punch into a 1-quart bottle. Seal and refrigerate until chilled.

4. Pour each serving into a chilled rocks glass over a large ice cube (preferably one that's clear; see Clear Ice on page 54). Store any leftover punch in the fridge for months or even years.

CLARIFIED MILK PUNCH

Okay, so we just learned a recipe that involves curdling milk. Most people's first reaction to this is a mixture of confusion and disgust, and I don't blame them. It's weird, there's some science involved that is unintuitive, and well, you're curdling milk. The technique is similar to making a consommé, a clear soup that uses egg whites to congeal solids before straining them out. I'll try to explain in simple terms what is happening when you clarify milk punches, justify why you should definitely make them, and provide a rough template for turning your favorite cocktails into milk punches.

The citric acid in your punch will cause the milk to curdle, causing the milk proteins to bind with astringent flavors of the punch, such as tea or oak tannins.

WHAT IS HAPPENING WHEN YOU CLARIFY A COCKTAIL WITH MILK?

When the acid from lime or lemon juice interacts with the milk it causes the milk to curdle. When the milk curdles, the casein proteins in the milk will bind to astringent-tasting tannins present in the cocktail, whether they are oak tannins from aged spirits like whiskey or tannins from tea or red wine. (Science-y side note: Tannins are a class of polyphenol molecules, and these are specifically what bind with the milk proteins.) The proteins will also bind to the cloudiness-inducing particles of the drink.

So now that we've created a nest of curdled milk that's bound to astringent tannins and cloudy particles, we want to filter those out. Running the punch through a coffee filter has given me the best results, but note that it could take several hours to complete the filtering process. Luckily, almost all of that time is hands off.

The filtering process will also remove some of the color and cloudiness of the cocktail, while leaving behind the whey proteins from the milk.

Filtering out the curdled milk will result in a clear, flavorful punch with a wonderfully rich mouthfeel.

WHY BOTHER MAKING A CLARIFIED MILK PUNCH?

First and foremost, these milk punches taste amazing. By stripping out the astringent tannins, the flavors left behind are more mellow and smooth. Moreover, the remaining whey proteins in the drink create a luscious mouthfeel that is just delightful.

Beyond taste, clarified milk punches look beautiful. Pour them over a clear ice cube (see Clear Ice on page 54) and watch the cube disappear in the cocktail. Clarified milk punches also help prevent the cocktail from spoiling so it can last years (yes, years) in the fridge.

A STANDARD TEMPLATE FOR MILK PUNCHES

Using one basic set of steps, you can turn any sour cocktail into a milk punch. Here are a few pointers:

- Do this with a batch of cocktails instead of individual drinks since it's labor intensive.

- The general rule of thumb is to use 1 part milk to 4 parts of your batched cocktail (e.g., if you start with 20 ounces of your batched cocktail, you'll need 5 ounces of milk).

- While whole cow milk is standard, you can also use whole goat milk for a little tang, sheep milk, or regular coconut milk. (The lack of natural fat content in nut milks means they won't work well for clarifying.)

- I prefer clarifying with cold milk to hot milk, though this is a vigorously debated topic. I've had nothing but success with cold milk.

- Pour the punch into the milk to curdle, not the other way around. This slows the curdling process and gives more time for the proteins to bind.

Basic Clarified Milk Punch Template

SCALE UP AS DESIRED

1 part cold whole milk

2 parts spirit (ideally an aged spirit)

1 part fresh lime or lemon juice

1 part simple syrup (page 14)

1. Add the milk to a large nonreactive bowl and set aside.

2. Combine the remaining ingredients in a pitcher and stir together. Slowly pour into the milk and gently stir until it curdles. Strain through a coffee filter into a large bowl (this could take a couple hours) and discard the filter.

3. Funnel the clarified milk punch into a bottle. Seal and refrigerate until chilled.

4. Pour each serving into a rocks glass over a large ice cube (preferably one that's clear; see Clear Ice on page 54). Store any leftover punch in the fridge for months or even years.

RELATED

CLARIFIED PIÑA COLADA

**MAKES ABOUT
4 SERVINGS**

5½ ounces (165 ml) cold whole milk

8 ounces (240 ml) aged rum

6 ounces (180 ml) coconut water

4 ounces (120 ml) strained fresh pineapple juice

2 ounces (60 ml) strained fresh lime juice

2 ounces (60 ml) simple syrup (page 14)

Back when I was experimenting with different cocktails to turn into milk punches, the piña colada was at the top of my list. I was amazed at how well it worked, and I finished the whole bottle in one sitting. I guess vacation mode set in right away. Note: Strain out the pulp from the pineapple and lime juices to improve clarity and make the filtering process easier.

1. Add the milk to a large nonreactive bowl and set aside.

2. Combine the remaining ingredients in a pitcher and stir together. Slowly pour into the milk and gently stir until it curdles. Strain through a coffee filter into a large bowl (this could take a couple hours) and discard the filter.

3. Funnel the clarified milk punch into a 1-quart bottle. Seal and refrigerate until chilled.

4. Pour each serving into a rocks glass over a large ice cube (preferably one that's clear; see Clear Ice on page 54). Store any leftover punch in the fridge for months or even years.

PAN GALACTIC GARGLE BLASTER

and other rapid infusions

In *The Hitchhiker's Guide to the Galaxy*, a comedy science fiction series created by Douglas Adams, the Pan Galactic Gargle Blaster is considered to be the "best drink in existence." This was a particularly fun cocktail to recreate, as many of the ingredients are fictional.

One of the challenging instructions in the original text was to pass through the drink "Fallian marsh gas," a substance that supposedly caused many happy hikers to die of pleasure. So, I employed a culinary technique called "rapid infusion" that involves N_2O (aka laughing gas) and a whipping siphon.

I came up with the following specs for this drink, with each ingredient representing the corresponding fictional ingredient (in parentheses) from the original text.

1. Grab your towel. Add the vodka, saline solution, gin, and lemon zest to a 1-pint (½-liter) iSi whipper.

2. Charge the whipper with one of the N_2O canisters, according to the manufacturer's directions, and shake. Repeat with the second N_2O canister and shake. Let sit for 2 minutes. Hold the whipper upright and vent rapidly into a cup and over a bowl to catch any liquid.

3. Remove the cap from the whipper and let the infusion sit for a few more minutes while the trapped gas bubbles and extracts more of the flavors. Strain the drink through a fine-mesh strainer into a mixing glass; discard the solids. Float the crème de menthe on top, slowly pouring it over the back of a spoon. Dash the sugar cube with your Firewater Tincture and drop into the mixing glass. Stir with ice for about 60 seconds. Double strain (pour through a Hawthorne strainer over the fine-mesh strainer) into a chilled stemless martini glass. Sprinkle the citric acid on top and stir with the olive on the cocktail pick. "Drink . . . but . . . very carefully."

RECREATED

MAKES 1 DRINK

1½ ounces (42 ml) vodka (Ol' Janx Spirit)

3 drops 20% saline solution (page 19; Santraginean seawater)

1½ ounces (42 ml) navy strength gin (Arcturan Mega-gin)

0.18 ounce (5 g) finely grated lemon zest (from about 2 lemons)

2 iSi N_2O chargers (Fallian marsh gas)

¼ ounce (7 ml) white crème de menthe (Qualactin Hypermint extract)

1 sugar cube

1 dash Scrappy's Firewater Tincture bitters (tooth of an Algolian Suntiger)

½ teaspoon (2 g) citric acid (Zamphuor)

1 green olive, skewered on a cocktail pick, for garnish

RAPID INFUSIONS

HOW DOES IT WORK?

Whipping siphons create a high-pressure environment in the vessel by using compressed nitrous oxide (N_2O) to aerate liquids and turn them into foams or creams. But if we throw some porous solids into a whipping siphon along with a spirit, this same pressure will force the liquid into the pores of the solid. Then when we rapidly discharge the gas, the liquid will pull out those flavors from the solid and become infused with the aromas.

Solids that work well for rapid infusion are porous ingredients, like fresh herbs, citrus zest, coffee beans, peppers, ginger, or cocoa nibs. Again, this is because they have pores for the liquid to pass through

Infusing flavors of fruits, fresh peppers, or coffee into spirits is a great way to riff on classic cocktails, but sometimes these infusions can take hours or days to be potent enough for use. Enter "rapid infusion," which trims that infusion time from days to minutes. The catch is that you need a whipping siphon, and ideally a high-quality one, such as the iSi brand. Chefs and bartenders traditionally used whipping siphons to make creams and foams, but culinary and cocktail scientist Dave Arnold discovered this genius technique that yields bright, delicious infusions on demand.

1. Use a pint-size (½-liter) iSi whipper for this technique and don't exceed 17 ounces (500 ml) of liquid.

in the high-pressure environment. Solids that won't work are powders, since they will clog your device, and nonporous solids that won't take in the liquid.

I use a pint-size (½-liter) iSi whipper to ensure enough room for all the liquid, add in up to a pint of spirit or vermouth, and then drop in my solid ingredients. The amount of solids will vary depending on the ingredient, but in general you will use more solids compared to a normal infusion technique. I then typically use two N_2O chargers (ensuring the iSi whipper is properly sealed) to maximize the pressure and let it rest for 1 to 2 minutes to allow time for the flavors to be extracted. I then always discharge the gas quickly and with the nozzle upright, as we aren't trying to discharge the liquid. If your whipper container is more than half full, some liquid might sputter out along with the gas, so you may need to hold a cup over the nozzle and discharge over a bowl to catch any liquid.

After you dispel all the gas, remove the cap from the whipper, and let the infusion sit for a few more minutes while the trapped gas bubbles and extracts more of the flavors. Then strain out and discard the solids. Use the infusion right away or store in an airtight container in the fridge, where it will retain its brightness for about a week. After that the flavors will fade.

2. Hold the whipper upright and discharge the gas rapidly to extract more flavor, with a cup over the nozzle just in case any liquid comes out.

3. Strain out and discard the solids. Try to use the infusion within a week, while the flavor is strongest.

GINGER MARGARITA

Ginger is an excellent ingredient to use for the rapid infusion technique since it's both porous and flavorful. It also happens to pair very well with tequila. So, I decided to infuse blanco tequila with ginger to use in the classic three-ingredient Tommy's Margarita. When making a cocktail with an infusion, I like to keep the rest of the drink fairly simple to really showcase the flavor from the infusion.

MAKES 1 DRINK

2 ounces (60 ml) Ginger-Infused Tequila (recipe follows)

1 ounce (30 ml) fresh lime juice

½ ounce (15 ml) agave syrup

3 pieces of candied ginger, skewered on a cocktail pick, for garnish

Add the tequila, lime juice, and agave syrup to a shaker tin with ice and shake for 15 seconds. Double strain (pour through a Hawthorne strainer over a fine-mesh strainer) into a chilled coupe. Garnish with the candied ginger and serve.

Ginger-Infused Tequila

MAKES 15 OUNCES (450 ML)

17 ounces (500 ml) blanco tequila

3.5 ounces (100 g) fresh peeled ginger, sliced into $\frac{1}{10}$-inch (2-mm) thick disks

2 iSi N_2O chargers

1. Add the tequila and ginger to a 1-pint (½-liter) iSi whipper. Charge the whipper with one of the N_2O canisters, according to the manufacturer's directions, and shake. Repeat with the second N_2O canister. Let sit for 2 minutes. Hold the whipper upright and vent rapidly into a cup and over a bowl to catch any liquid.

2. Remove the cap from the whipper and let the infusion sit for a few more minutes while the trapped gas bubbles and extracts more of the flavors. Strain the infusion through a fine-mesh strainer into a liquid measuring cup; discard the solids. Pour the infused tequila into a 1-pint bottle and use right away or seal and store in the fridge. Best if consumed within a week, otherwise the flavor fades.

CACAO BOULEVARDIER

RELATED

Cacao nibs are another great option for the rapid infusion technique. They're simply crushed up cacao beans that are often dry roasted. Cacao nibs aren't sweet but have a rich chocolate flavor that pairs well with sweet vermouth and dark spirits, so if you like Boulevardiers and chocolate, you'll love this drink. Side note: Try using the infused vermouth in a Manhattan (page 105) as well to get more mileage out of it!

Add the vermouth, Campari, and rye to a mixing glass with ice and stir for about 45 seconds. Strain into a rocks glass over a large ice cube (preferably one that's clear; see Clear Ice on page 54). Squeeze the orange twist to express the essential oils over the drink, drop in the twist, and serve.

Cacao-Infused Sweet Vermouth

1. Add the vermouth and cacao nibs to a 1-pint (½-liter) iSi whipper. Charge the whipper with one of the N_2O canisters, according to the manufacturer's directions, and shake. Repeat with the second N_2O canister. Let sit for 30 seconds. Hold the whipper upright and vent rapidly into a cup and over a bowl to catch any liquid.

2. Remove the cap from the whipper and let the infusion sit for a few more minutes while the trapped gas bubbles and extracts more of the flavors. Strain the infusion through a fine-mesh strainer into a liquid measuring cup; discard the solids. Pour the infused vermouth into a 1-pint bottle and use right away or seal and store in the fridge. Best if consumed within a week, otherwise the flavor fades.

MAKES 1 DRINK

1 ounce (30 ml) Cacao-Infused Sweet Vermouth (recipe follows)

1 ounce (30 ml) Campari

1 ounce (30 ml) rye

1 orange twist, for garnish

MAKES 15 OUNCES (450 ML)

17 ounces (500 ml) sweet vermouth

3.5 ounces (100 g) cacao nibs

2 iSi N_2O chargers

ONE OF EVERYTHING
and other loaded cocktails

Michael Scott from the American TV show *The Office* is a master paper salesman, the king of cringe, and occasionally plays the office mixologist. He's a man who knows what he likes, and what he likes is the artificial sweetener Splenda, especially when paired with a twenty-year-old single malt Scotch. While I did consider his signature Scotch and Splenda cocktail for this book, his truly innovative concoction came in season five during a "Moroccan Christmas" party.

Never has Michael looked so confident behind the bar as when he presented his original One of Everything cocktail to his colleagues. An equal parts cocktail of six (yes, six) different types of booze served in a gold plastic cup, the One of Everything rounds out its rough edges with a couple packets of Splenda. Here's the recipe, but be forewarned, this drink is worse than Toby Flenderson.

Add all the ingredients to a short gold plastic cup. Stir. Sip. Spit out.

RECREATED

MAKES 1 "DRINK"

¾ ounce (22 ml) Scotch

¾ ounce (22 ml) absinthe

¾ ounce (22 ml) white rum

¾ ounce (22 ml) gin

¾ ounce (22 ml) sweet vermouth

¾ ounce (22 ml) triple sec

2 packets of Splenda

RELATED

LONG ISLAND ICED TEA

MAKES 1 DRINK

½ ounce (15 ml) white rum

½ ounce (15 ml) vodka

½ ounce (15 ml) gin

½ ounce (15 ml) reposado tequila

½ ounce (15 ml) triple sec

¾ ounce (22 ml) fresh lemon juice

¼ ounce (7 ml) simple syrup (page 14)

1½ ounces (45 ml) chilled cola

On the topic of loaded cocktails with a variety of spirits, nothing rivals the LIIT. Born in the 1970s, this drink really has one of everything along with a reputation of sending you to the moon. My version of the Long Island Iced Tea is within the standard range of ABV for cocktails, coming in at 20% alcohol, but it still has more booze than the average drink. More important, it's absolutely delicious and despite not having any iced tea, it tastes strikingly similar. If you're trying to clear out some bottles from your liquor cabinet, look no further than this recipe.

Add all the ingredients except the cola to a shaker tin with ice. Shake for 15 seconds. Double strain (pour through a Hawthorne strainer over a fine-mesh strainer) into a Collins glass with ice (preferably a clear ice stick; see Clear Ice on page 54). Top with the cola, stir with a spoon straw, and serve.

AMF (ADIOS MOTHERF***KER)

The AMF is a variation on the Long Island Iced Tea (page 78), simply replacing the triple sec with blue Curaçao (which is just a blue-colored triple sec), and the cola with lemon-lime soda. Do I make a lot of these at the home bar? No, but beautiful blue cocktails are one of my guilty pleasures.

Add all the ingredients except the soda to a shaker tin with ice. Shake for 15 seconds. Double strain (pour through a Hawthorne strainer over a fine-mesh strainer) into a Collins glass with ice (preferably a clear ice stick; see Clear Ice on page 54). Top with the soda, garnish with a tiki umbrella, and serve.

MAKES 1 DRINK

½ ounce (15 ml) white rum

½ ounce (15 ml) vodka

½ ounce (15 ml) gin

½ ounce (15 ml) blanco tequila

½ ounce (15 ml) blue Curaçao

¾ ounce (22 ml) fresh lemon juice

¼ ounce (7 ml) simple syrup (page 14)

1½ ounces (45 ml) chilled lemon-lime soda

THANKS-TINI

and other fall cocktails

RECREATED

MAKES 1 DRINK

---

2 ounces (60 ml) potato vodka

4 ounces (120 ml) chilled cranberry juice

1 chicken bouillon cube

Barney Stinson from the TV show *How I Met Your Mother* is a man of confidence. A serial womanizer, he spends much of the series using that confidence for elaborate acts of seduction. But in season one that same confidence leads to what is perhaps the most bold cocktail invention in TV history: the Thanks-tini, Barney's attempt to create a drink that "tastes just like a turkey dinner." Allow me to set the scene here, because it is a true act of cocktail innovation.

Barney and the gang are out at a restaurant, their martini glasses filled with cranberry-vodka cocktails that they presumably ordered from the establishment. So, we now have a few familiar staples of the American Thanksgiving meal in cocktail form: cranberries in the juice, and potatoes (used to distill the vodka). But Barney then adds one final ingredient. He grabs a few bouillon cubes from a large container that he himself brought to the table and drops one in each glass in a move that can only be described as "legen . . . wait for it . . . dary."

Boldness aside, the drink has some flaws. First, potato vodka won't remind you of Thanksgiving mashed potatoes since it's distilled from a potato mash and doesn't actually taste like spuds. More important, that bouillon cube is not going to dissolve easily in a cold beverage. Even after muddling, the pieces just sink to the bottom of the glass in a salty mess. Still want me to help you recreate this? Challenge accepted.

Add the vodka and cranberry juice to a shaker tin with ice. Shake for 15 seconds. Double strain (pour through a Hawthorne strainer over a fine-mesh strainer) into a chilled martini glass. Add the bouillon cube and muddle to incorporate, as much as possible. Drink and feel your blood pressure rise from all that sodium.

IMPROVED THANKS-TINI

RELATED

MAKES 1 DRINK

1 ounce (30 ml) London dry gin

1 ounce (30 ml) ruby port

½ ounce (15 ml) pure maple syrup

¾ ounce (22 ml) fresh lemon juice

1 heaping barspoon jellied cranberry sauce (15 g)

1 small fresh sage sprig, for garnish

To make my improved version of this drink I started brainstorming some iconic fall flavors, like cranberry, cinnamon, maple, red wine, and sage. I wanted to use some ruby port, which often makes its way into fall cocktails, as it is a fortified dessert wine that has red berry and cinnamon flavors. I felt like gin would also pair well with the sage and cranberry, but you could reach for whiskey instead if you prefer dark spirits (maybe Wild Turkey?).

I loved how this recipe turned out, and it's now part of my regular fall cocktail rotation.

Add the gin, port, maple syrup, lemon juice, and cranberry sauce to a shaker tin with ice. Shake for 15 seconds and double strain (pour through a Hawthorne strainer over a fine-mesh strainer) into a rocks glass over crushed ice. Clap the sage between your hands to release the aroma (see Note) then garnish the drink with it. Enjoy with good friends and family.

As with clapping mint and other fragrant herbs, clapping your hands together with a sage sprig in between them will release its essential oils and greatly enhance the aroma.

PUMPKIN SPICE COCKTAIL

RELATED

Okay, yes, it might be basic, but a homemade pumpkin spice syrup is delicious and an easy way to add autumnal flavor to cocktails. I make a batch of this syrup every year and swap it in place of simple syrup in a variety of cocktails, such as an Irish Coffee (page 105) or Old Fashioned (page 52). So, let's learn how to use this syrup in a whiskey sour to turn it into a delicious fall cocktail that pairs well with flannel and a North Face jacket.

MAKES 1 DRINK

2 ounces (60 ml) whiskey

¾ ounce (22 ml) Pumpkin Spice Syrup (recipe follows)

¾ ounce (22 ml) fresh lemon juice

Add the whiskey, pumpkin spice syrup, and lemon juice to a shaker tin with ice. Shake for 15 seconds. Double strain (pour through a Hawthorne strainer over a fine-mesh strainer) into a chilled coupe and serve.

Pumpkin Spice Syrup

1. Add the sugar and water to a small saucepan and bring to a boil. Turn down the heat to a simmer, add the pumpkin and spices, and stir together. Let simmer for 10 minutes. Remove from the heat and let cool for 20 minutes.

2. Strain through a fine-mesh sieve lined with a nut milk bag or cheesecloth into a medium bowl. Discard the solids. Funnel the syrup into a bottle. Seal and store in the fridge for up to two weeks.

YIELDS 14 OUNCES (400 ML)

1½ cups (350 g) Demerara or light brown sugar

1½ cups (350 ml) water

¼ cup (65 g) canned pure pumpkin puree

4 cinnamon sticks (10 g) or 1 teaspoon (3 g) ground cinnamon

1½ teaspoons (3 g) ground ginger

1 teaspoon (2 g) ground cloves

½ teaspoon (1 g) freshly grated nutmeg

CUBA LIBRE

and other highball cocktails

The movie *Cocktail* (1988) showed what happens when you put Tom Cruise's manic energy at a high-volume bar in New York City or a beach bar in Jamaica. In addition to being universally panned by critics, the movie showcases the "dark ages" of cocktails in America, a time that favored flashiness and neon-colored drinks over quality. But before Cruise mastered his sick flair bartending moves, he got stumped by a classic highball: the Cuba Libre (or as the server called it, a "Cuba Libra").

Most people mistake this drink for a basic rum and Coke, but it contains one key enhancement that cannot be understated: fresh lime juice. The sweetness of the cola needs some balance, and adding a bit of acid really brightens up the drink.

So, Tom, give Iceman a call to fill up your highball glass and let's make a proper Cuba Libre.

Add the rum, lime juice, and cola to a rocks glass with ice. Stir to mix. Garnish with the lime wedge and serve.

RECREATED

MAKES 1 DRINK

2 ounces (60 ml) light rum

½ ounce (15 ml) fresh lime juice

4 ounces (120 ml) chilled cola

1 lime wedge, for garnish

IMPROVED CUBA LIBRE

RELATED

MAKES 1 DRINK

1 ounce (30 ml) light rum

¾ ounce (22 ml) Homemade Cola Syrup (recipe follows) or store-bought cola syrup

½ ounce (15 ml) strained fresh lemon juice

¼ ounce (7ml) Fernet-Branca

4 ounces (120 ml) chilled sparkling wine

1 half lemon wheel, for garnish

While the classic Cuba Libre (page 89) shouldn't be messed with, there's always space for innovation around the core ingredients. I decided to mix the drink with a homemade cola syrup instead of cola because that allows us to play with other forms of carbonation. The first time I tried a cola syrup in a cocktail was at BlackTail, a beautiful bar in New York City specializing in Cuban drinks that unfortunately closed in 2020. Taking inspiration from them, I simmer cola in a saucepan until it reduces to one-sixth of its volume to make the cola syrup (pro tip: pour cola into the saucepan and mark a toothpick at the liquid surface then use it to tell how far the cola has reduced) and replace the carbonation with sparkling wine. A touch of fernet, a type of bitter amaro, works wonderfully with cola (fernet and Coke is hugely popular in Argentina), so let's incorporate that as well.

Add the rum, cola syrup, lemon juice, and fernet to a Collins glass with ice (preferably a clear ice stick; see Clear Ice on page 54). Stir for 15 seconds to mix and chill the ingredients. Top with the sparkling wine. Garnish with the half lemon wheel and serve with a spoon straw.

Homemade Cola Syrup

MAKES 4 OUNCES (120 ML)

24 ounces (700 ml) cola

Add your target reduction volume of cola to a medium saucepan, in this case 4 ounces (120 ml). Stand a toothpick or wooden chopstick in the saucepan and mark it at the surface of the cola. Pour in the remaining cola and simmer over medium heat until it reduces down to where the toothpick is marked, about 15 minutes. Let cool to room temperature, then funnel the syrup into a small bottle. Seal and store in the fridge for up to one month.

MULES

Since you're reading this book, there's a decent chance you're known as that "cocktail person" in your social circle, meaning you're likely to be tapped to sling drinks at parties or events. That can be fun for a bit, but it can also be a drag. You could make a punch, but that's also a lot of work.

No surprise that I'm this guy, and I'm going to let you in on my secret to managing a constant flow of thirsty friends and family: mules. These days, a mule refers to a highball made with ginger beer and citrus (sometimes called a "buck" if made with ginger ale instead of ginger beer). Turns out, ginger beer is the ultimate crowd-pleaser. Most imbibing folk are happy to get a mule with quality ginger beer and the spirit of their choice.

But the real benefit of mules is how easy it is to adapt to a guest's preference. Pretty much any spirit works in this template. There's the Moscow Mule (made with vodka), the Kentucky Mule (made with bourbon), or my favorite, the Mezcal Mule (take a guess). Using a dark rum turns it into a Dark 'n Stormy, though you can only legally call it that if made with Goslings Black Seal rum because the producer trademarked the name. Real cool of you, guys.

But even more important is the type of ginger beer you use, considering it makes up the majority of the highball. I prefer something with a little kick, it is a mule after all, and I mostly reach for Fever-Tree or Q brand ginger beer.

For the lime, I skip the precise measurements and just hand squeeze the citrus directly into the glass. Mules are pretty forgiving drinks, so your craft mixology skills aren't needed here.

Still sound like too much work at a party? Just line up all the ingredients, leave a few instructions, and let your guests self-serve. Put out a tip jar while you're at it.

MAKES 1 DRINK

½ lime

2 ounces (60 ml) your spirit of choice

6 ounces (180 ml) chilled ginger beer (preferably a high-quality brand, such as Fever-Tree or Q)

Squeeze the juice from the lime into a Collins glass with ice. Add the spirit and top with the ginger beer. Drop in a spoon straw, give the drink a quick stir, and serve.

FIGHT MILK

and other flips

The TV sitcom *It's Always Sunny in Philadelphia* features a gang of misfits who run an unsuccessful bar called Paddy's Pub. Despite failing at most endeavors while being generally terrible human beings, their unwavering confidence has led to some rather innovative ways to consume alcohol, such as Riot Juice and Rum Ham.

But their Fight Milk is on another level. Touted as "the first alcoholic, dairy-based, protein drink made for bodyguards by bodyguards," it contains milk, a whole bunch of vodka, and high levels of "crowtein" from all the crow eggs that go into each batch. Perfect for muscular bodyguards who also want to get a buzz on, Don Draper couldn't have marketed it any better.

Since it's near impossible to come by crow eggs, I substituted regular chicken eggs to try and recreate this drink, and to be honest, it wasn't terrible. That's likely because the Fight Milk recipe stays pretty close to a classic cocktail template called a flip, which is made up of sugar, alcohol, and a whole egg.

Adding a whole egg to alcoholic drinks goes back centuries, and at one point it was common to plunge a hot poker into your beverage (then commonly made with beer) that caused it to froth around or "flip." These days, most flips are served cold and often with a fortified wine, like sherry or port, and they are delightful as the egg adds wonderful body and texture to the drink.

So, if you ironically want to recreate Fight Milk from the show, here's how I'd do it. But I'd also advise, just don't do it.

RECREATED

MAKES 13 DRINKS FOR BODYGUARDS

1 gallon (3.8 liters) whole milk

One (750-ml) bottle vodka

A dozen eggs

Add all of the ingredients to a large metal pot. Whisk the eggs until fully incorporated. Ladle a serving into a pint glass. Drink every morning so you can fight like a crow.

NEW YORK FLIP

MAKES 1 DRINK

1½ ounces (45 ml) bourbon

¾ ounce (22 ml) tawny port

¾ ounce heavy cream

¼ ounce (7 ml) simple syrup (page 14)

1 large egg yolk

Freshly grated nutmeg or cinnamon, for garnish

While not all flips contain dairy, some of my favorites mix in cream along with the egg to create a drink that's even more rich and decadent. If you're looking to make an improved Fight Milk (page 95), the New York Flip would be my go-to. This recipe is basically a New York Sour (page 139) but "flippified," replacing the lemon juice with egg and cream.

Add the bourbon, port, cream, and simple syrup to a shaker tin with ice. Shake for 15 seconds, then double strain (pour through a Hawthorne strainer over a fine-mesh strainer) into the shaker's smaller tin (or pint glass) and discard the ice. Add the egg yolk to the chilled cocktail and dry shake (shake without ice) for 15 seconds. Pour into a chilled coupe. Garnish with freshly grated nutmeg or cinnamon and serve.

SPIKED EGGNOG

Eggnog is a close cousin of the flip, and some would classify any flip with dairy as technically being a nog. Regardless of definition, if you want to treat yourself to a deliciously rich and creamy cocktail, make your own eggnog come holiday season over buying one that's premade. There is no shortage of recipes out there, and if you're looking for something that's easy to batch in the blender, I highly recommend bartender Jeffrey Morgenthaler's tequila and sherry version. It's become a sort of modern classic.

But if you're like me and need some self-control when it comes to spiked eggnog, I'd suggest shaking up a single serving at a time instead. Here is my preferred recipe, which has the benefit of being an equal parts cocktail so it's easy to remember. I like to split the base between rum and Cognac, but you can replace them with any dark spirit you like here.

Add the rum, Cognac, cream, and simple syrup to a shaker tin with ice. Shake for 15 seconds, then double strain (pour through a Hawthorne strainer over a fine-mesh strainer) into the shaker's smaller tin (or pint glass) and discard the ice. Add the egg to the chilled cocktail and dry shake (shake without ice) for 15 seconds. Pour into a chilled rocks glass. Grate nutmeg and cinnamon over the drink and serve.

MAKES 1 DRINK

1 ounce (30 ml) dark rum

1 ounce (30 ml) Cognac

1 ounce (30 ml) heavy cream

1 ounce (30 ml) simple syrup (page 14)

1 large egg

Freshly grated nutmeg, for garnish

Freshly grated cinnamon stick, for garnish

Freshly grated nutmeg and cinnamon will have a more intense aroma than the pre-ground versions.

BLACK YUKON SUCKER PUNCH

and other coffee cocktails

The TV show *Twin Peaks* ran for two seasons back in the early 1990s. It was classic David Lynch surrealism and, frankly, it's not my cup of tequila. But when it returned for a third season in 2017, it was the perfect opportunity to recreate a highly requested, blue-foamed cocktail from season two called the Black Yukon Sucker Punch. For the full *Twin Peaks* experience, I partnered up with Andrew Rea from the excellent YouTube channel *Binging with Babish* to pair this drink with the TV show's signature pancakes.

Add the whiskey and coffee to a heatproof Collins glass. Float the foam on top, slowly pouring it over the back of a spoon. Serve right away.

RECREATED

MAKES 1 DRINK

2 ounces (60 ml) whiskey

6 ounces (180 ml) fresh brewed hot black coffee

4 ounces (120 ml) Blue Foam (recipe follows)

Blue Foam

1. In a large bowl, beat the egg whites with an electric mixer on medium speed (or by hand) until stiff peaks form. Mix in the sugar just until combined. Set aside.

2. In a separate large bowl, whip the cream with an electric mixer on medium-high speed (or by hand) until stiff peaks form. Add the vanilla extract, salt, and 2 ounces of the blue Curaçao. Mix together on low speed until just combined, then mix in the remaining 2 ounces blue Curaçao. Fold in the egg whites. Use right away or store in an airtight container in the fridge until ready to use, up to three days.

MAKES ABOUT 40 OUNCES (ABOUT 1.2 LITERS; ENOUGH FOR 10 DRINKS)

3 large egg whites (see Note on page 128)

¼ cup (50 g) sugar

1 cup (236 ml) heavy whipping cream

1 teaspoon (5 ml) pure vanilla extract

¼ teaspoon (1.5 g) kosher salt

4 ounces (120 ml) blue Curaçao

RELATED

IRISH COFFEE

MAKES 1 DRINK

4 ounces (120 ml) fresh brewed hot coffee

1½ ounces (45 ml) Irish whiskey

¾ ounce (22 ml) Demerara syrup (see simple syrup, page 14)

1 ounce (30 ml) heavy cream

Freshly grated nutmeg, for garnish (optional)

If you're a fan of combining coffee and cocktails like I am but can't be bothered to make that blue foam in the Black Yukon Sucker Punch (page 101), just stick to the tried-and-true Irish Coffee. On the surface it appears to be a simple drink: just coffee, sugar, whiskey, and cream. But I've had a wide range of quality with this hot cocktail, and I've come up with the perfect recipe.

First and most important, brew some high-quality drip coffee. It is the majority of the drink so don't skimp on this ingredient. Opt for freshly roasted and ground beans, brewed whichever style you prefer (I'm a pour-over guy myself).

The whiskey should be Irish, of course. I'd choose a mid-range brand as the subtleties of a well-aged whiskey will be completely lost here.

For the sugar, most add a couple of plain white sugar cubes. But for a more complex and rich flavor, I'd opt for a light brown sugar syrup or Demerara syrup.

And finally, the cream. I prefer an unsweetened heavy cream freshly whipped until it's thick enough to be layered on top of the drink while still thin enough to free pour instead of scoop. Pro tip: Instead of dirtying another tool, simply whip the cream by shaking it vigorously in a cocktail shaker.

1. Fill a Georgian Irish coffee glass with hot water then dump it out. Add the coffee, whiskey, and Demerara syrup. Give it a quick stir.

2. Add the cream to a shaker tin and shake vigorously until thick and pourable, about 45 seconds. Layer the whipped cream on top of the drink, slowly pouring it over the back of a spoon. Grate nutmeg on top, if using, and serve right away.

102   COCKTAIL CHEMISTRY

POURING COCKTAILS THROUGH COFFEE

In the morning I pour water through ground beans to make coffee. At night I pour spirits through a strainer to make a cocktail. And like the first person to simultaneously hold a chocolate bar and a peanut butter jar, I was about to have a eureka moment.

What if we poured the cocktail through the ground coffee to flavor the drink? Cue fireworks, air horns, and vuvuzelas; we have a winner.

There were some details to work out. How fine should the coffee grounds be? Which cocktails does this work best with? Do you chill the cocktail with ice before or after straining through the coffee?

For the last question, I challenged fellow YouTuber and coffee guru James Hoffman to test both options, and he came to the same conclusion I did: Chill the cocktail before pouring through coffee. The warmer the liquid, the more coffee flavor gets extracted into the final product. So, if you start with a room temperature cocktail, the coffee flavor becomes too dominant. You're going for subtle undertones here.

This technique tends to work best with spirit-forward cocktails using darker spirits, but I'd encourage you to experiment with your own pour-overs. Take your favorite cocktail and see how it works.

I find that 15 grams of dark roast coffee at a medium-fine grind (setting 14 on my Encore burr grinder) provides the perfect amount of coffee flavor.

MANHATTAN POUR-OVER

Most spirit-forward cocktails made using dark spirits will shine with this technique, so let's start with the classic Manhattan. Note that there will be about a 10 percent loss of cocktail that is held back in the coffee grounds, so feel free to scale up the recipe as you see fit.

1. Place a wet paper filter into a pour-over coffee dripper and add the ground coffee. Set aside.

2. Add the rye, vermouth, Angostura bitters, and the walnut bitters, if using, to a mixing glass with ice. Stir for about 45 seconds. Place the prepared pour-over dripper on top of a chilled coupe. Slowly pour the cocktail over the coffee grounds in a steady spiral toward the outer edge and then back toward the center to agitate the coffee and obtain an even extraction. Allow the cocktail to drip into the coupe. Garnish with the maraschino cherry and serve.

MAKES 1 DRINK

1½ ounces (15 g) dark roast coffee beans, ground medium-fine

2 ounces (60 ml) rye

1 ounce (30 ml) sweet vermouth

2 dashes Angostura bitters

2 dashes black walnut bitters (optional)

1 maraschino cherry, for garnish (I typically use Luxardo brand)

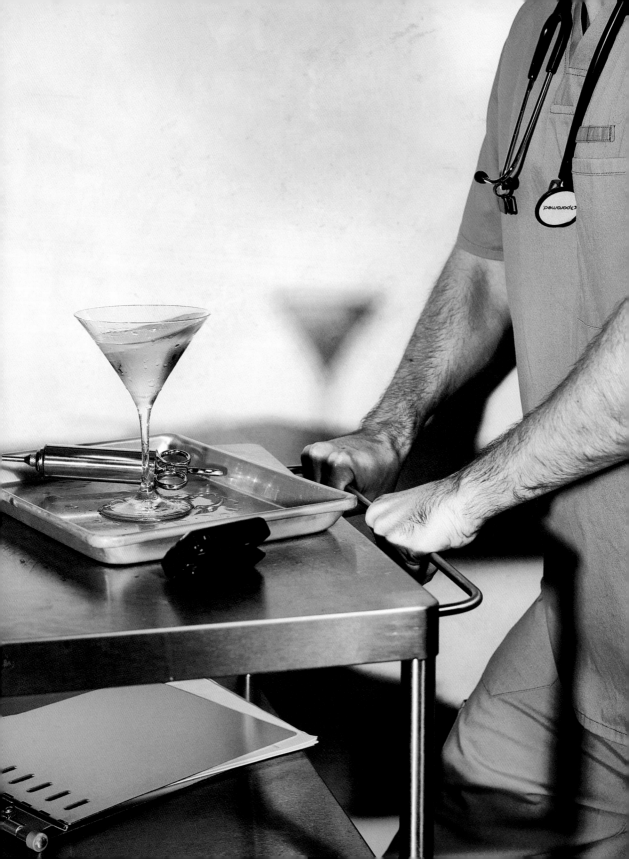

EASY ON THE TINI APPLETINI

and other "dark ages" cocktails

RECREATED

MAKES 1 DRINK

---

2 ounces (60 ml) DeKuyper Sour Apple Pucker or other green apple schnapps

1 ounce (30 ml) vodka

Throughout this book I make references to the "dark ages" of cocktails, generally defined by overly sweet drinks with artificial flavors and bright colors that served purely as fuel to a fun night. Nothing wrong with that, and I firmly believe cocktails should be fun and not taken so seriously. However, the period stretching from roughly the 1960s through the 1990s in America was a distinctly different cocktail era than the craft cocktail revival that followed.

The appletini came about during the 1990s in the death throes of these "dark ages" and began as a simple combination of radioactive neon-green sour apple schnapps and vodka in a martini glass. This drink had just enough time to hit mainstream when the TV show *Scrubs* aired in 2001. Zach Braff plays a young attending physician named J.D. who has a penchant for appletinis that are "easy on the tini." When ordering these at the bar, a public shaming at his "girly" choice of drink is sure to follow, but that never stops J.D.

I like the underlying message here: Drink what you like. Sweet drinks aren't feminine, spirit-forward drinks are not inherently masculine. Anyone who argues otherwise is likely battling some insecurities, so be like J.D. and even get sugar on the rim if you want.

So here is my interpretation of J.D.'s preferred appletini, with "easy on the tini" meaning heavier on the apple flavor. If you're into green apple Jolly Ranchers, this is the drink for you.

Add both ingredients to a shaker tin with ice. Shake for 15 seconds. Double-strain (pour through a Hawthorne strainer over a fine-mesh strainer) into a chilled martini glass and serve.

RELATED

IMPROVED APPLETINI

MAKES 1 DRINK

½ ounce (15 ml) fresh lemon juice

½ ounce (15 ml) simple syrup (page 14)

2 slices Granny Smith apple, plus 1 more for garnish

1½ ounces (45 ml) vodka

½ ounce (15 ml) sour apple liqueur (I use Leopold Bros. New York sour apple liqueur)

Fortunately, these days there are plenty of delicious alternatives to Sour Apple Pucker to get a natural apple flavor into your cocktail. One option is to use an applejack, which is an apple brandy that uses a process called "jacking" to freeze fermented cider then removing the ice to increase the alcohol content.

To get the sour apple flavor I wanted, I went with fresh Granny Smith apples and Leopold Bros., one of my trusted brands that produces an excellent sour apple liqueur. Here's how I make a delicious appletini with them.

1. Add the lemon juice, simple syrup, and 2 apple slices to a shaker tin. Muddle to extract the apple juice. Add the vodka and sour apple liqueur and shake with ice for 15 seconds.

2. Double strain (pour through a Hawthorne strainer over a fine-mesh strainer) into a chilled Nick & Nora glass. Garnish with the remaining apple slice.

HARVEY WALLBANGER

RELATED

One of the reasons I have such a mistrust of cocktail origin stories is the Harvey Wallbanger. This massively popular drink in the 1970s had a very specific and detailed backstory involving a Manhattan Beach surfer named Tom Harvey who got drunk and started running into walls. This story has been largely debunked; the drink was actually the creation of cocktail consultant Donato "Duke" Antone for the importing company that handled the signature ingredient, Galliano (a sweet herbal liqueur with heavy vanilla notes). It's not uncommon for a brand to partner with bartenders to create signature drinks, but rarely do they take off like the Harvey Wallbanger did. There was even a cringey ad campaign featuring a dopey cartoon surfer that you just need to look up for yourself. It's awful.

But this was a different time, and dopey fun was certainly in line with how cocktails were treated then. So, if you want a throwback, go pick up the obnoxiously tall bottle of Galliano and make the Harvey Wallbanger.

MAKES 1 DRINK

1½ ounces (45 ml) vodka

3 ounces (90 ml) fresh orange juice

½ ounce (15 ml) Galliano

1 maraschino cherry, for garnish

1 half orange wheel, for garnish

Stir the vodka and orange juice together with ice in a Collins glass. Float the Galliano on top, slowly pouring it over the back of a spoon. Garnish with the cherry and orange wheel. Bang head against wall.

FORGET-ME-SHOT

and other shots

Homer Simpson and Moe the bartender have a rich history of creating innovative drinks, including the famous Flaming Homer (page 169) that Moe ripped off and renamed the Flaming Moe. But as it turns out, Moe is quite the cocktail alchemist himself as we learn in season nineteen of the TV show when Homer is introduced to Moe's Forget-Me-Shot. According to Moe, "This drink is the ultimate brain bleacher, one swig wipes out the last day of your life"—the perfect way for Homer to purge the memory of discovering his surprise birthday party plans.

Recreating this recipe was actually quite similar to the Pan Galactic Gargle Blaster (page 71) since I had to get creative with some fictional ingredients. The first three ingredients are real, the rest are fictional or just too gross to attempt (leave your dog alone). You're not going to make this drink at home, but here's how I did it:

Add all of the ingredients to a large shot glass. Stir with a home pregnancy test stick until it turns positive (it won't). Shoot. Realize you were going to make a Forget-Me-Shot and repeat the above steps in a *Groundhog Day*–esque loop until you pass out.

RECREATED

MAKES 1 SHOT

¼ ounce (7 ml) Jägermeister

¼ ounce (7 ml) sloe gin

¼ ounce (7 ml) triple sec

¼ ounce (7 ml) triple sec with a few drops each of orange flower water and orange bitters (for the "quadruple sec")

Pinch of kosher salt (for the gunk from a dog's eye)

1 barspoon (5 ml) vodka plus 1 barspoon (5 ml) pickle brine (for the Absolut Pikl)

1 pea-size glob of the red stripe from Aquafresh toothpaste

Drop of extra-spicy hot sauce (for the venom of the Louisiana lobato-mouth)

PICKLEBACK SHOT

MAKES 1 SHOT

1½ ounces (45 ml) whiskey

1½ ounces (45 ml) chilled pickle brine

In 2006, a young Cocktail Chemist had just graduated college and was living in Manhattan, right when the modern cocktail renaissance was starting to take hold. But across the East River in Brooklyn, a revolutionary new shot was gaining traction that threatened to send us all back to the dark ages. It was called the pickleback shot, seemingly terrible but actually amazing. It's brilliant in its simplicity: a shot of whiskey chased by a shot of pickle brine.

The concept of pairing booze and salt isn't new. Russians have been consuming pickles with vodka for ages, salt and tequila is a college staple, and legend has it that long-haul truckers in Texas would chase whiskey with pickle brine to fend off bathroom breaks on the road since the salt retains liquid. Nice one, Texas.

Pickle brine is actually delicious and tempers the burn of the whiskey almost immediately. If you like pickles, give this one a shot (heh).

Add the whiskey to a shot glass. Add the pickle brine to another shot glass. Shoot the whiskey. Chase with the pickle brine.

50/50 AMARO SHOTS

The Forget-Me-Shot (page 113) includes Jägermeister, the notorious German bittersweet liqueur that I place into the broader category of amaro (Italian for "bitter"). And if we're talking about shots with amaro, we can't gloss over the 50/50 shots that have become a sort of "bartender's handshake." These shots started as a shift drink among bartenders and are typically equal parts amaro and another ingredient.

You can pour these straight into a shot glass or, as I prefer, stir the two ingredients over ice and strain into a glass. I absolutely love 50/50s; they're perfect for an after-dinner digestif or a post-party send off. Here are a few of my favorites.

RELATED

Ferrari

MAKES 1 SHOT

¾ ounce (22 ml) Fernet-Branca

¾ ounce (22 ml) Campari

Add the fernet and Campari to a mixing glass with ice. Stir and strain into a chilled shot glass. Shoot.

Black Fernet

MAKES 1 SHOT

¾ ounce (22 ml) Fernet-Branca

¾ ounce (22 ml) coffee liqueur (I prefer Mr Black cold brew coffee liqueur)

Add the fernet and coffee liqueur to a mixing glass with ice. Stir and strain into a chilled shot glass. Shoot.

Maserati

MAKES 1 SHOT

¾ ounce (22 ml) mezcal

¾ ounce (22 ml) Ramazzotti amaro

Add the mezcal and Ramazzotti to a mixing glass with ice. Stir and strain into a chilled shot glass. Shoot.

BUTTERBEER

and other fat washing and foam techniques

If you're in the mood to celebrate after an intense Quidditch match, nothing beats a frothy mug of butterbeer at the Three Broomsticks pub. While J.K. Rowling didn't provide an exact recipe in her Harry Potter book series, we do have some clues. She is on the record saying she made up the drink, which means it is distinct from the sixteenth-century beverage called "buttered beer" involving, well, butter and beer. She also imagined it to taste like "a less sickly butterscotch." My recreation of this drink is modeled after the warm version we see served in the movie *Harry Potter and the Half-Blood Prince*, and it is an excellent opportunity to experiment with two fun techniques: fat washing and creating foams. Here's the full recipe, and afterward I go into more detail about these techniques.

Add the bourbon and spiced apple cider to a warmed Irish coffee mug. Stir together, top with the foam, and serve.

RECREATED

MAKES 1 DRINK

---

2 ounces (60 ml) Brown Butter–Washed Bourbon (page 120)

4 ounces (120 ml) Spiced Apple Cider (page 120), heated

Butterscotch Foam (page 121), for topping

Brown Butter–Washed Bourbon

**MAKES 20 OUNCES
(ABOUT 600 ML)**

15 tablespoons (210 g)
unsalted butter

22 ounces (650 ml)
bourbon

1. Melt the butter in a small skillet or saucepan over medium heat and cook, stirring occasionally, until browned with a nutty aroma, 5 to 6 minutes. Pour the brown butter into a large freezer-safe bowl and add the bourbon. Cover and let infuse for an hour, agitating it frequently. Put in the freezer until the butter solidifies, about 30 minutes.

2. Using a small knife, pierce a hole in the layer of butter. Strain the bourbon through a sieve lined with coffee filters into a medium bowl. Store the brown butter–washed bourbon in a jar in the refrigerator and use within a few days.

Spiced Apple Cider

**MAKES 48 OUNCES
(1.5 LITERS)**

½ gallon (2 liters) apple
cider

4 cinnamon sticks

5 whole cloves

1½ teaspoons (2 g) whole
allspice

1 teaspoon (2 g) freshly
grated nutmeg

1 vanilla bean, split
lengthwise and seeds
scraped

1. Add the apple cider, cinnamon, cloves, allspice, nutmeg, and vanilla bean and seeds to a large pot. Bring to just a simmer over medium heat. Decrease the heat to medium-low and simmer until the cider reduces by about 25 percent, about 1 hour.

2. Strain the cider through a sieve lined with a nut milk bag or cheesecloth into a large heatproof bowl; discard the solids. Serve hot. Store any leftover cider in an airtight container in the refrigerator for up to two weeks.

Butterscotch Foam

1. Combine the schnapps, water, and bitters in a liquid measuring cup. Add half of the liquid to a small saucepan, reserving the rest for later. Drop the gelatin into the saucepan and warm over low heat until the gelatin is softened, about 5 minutes. Then heat the liquid to at least 98.6°F (37°C), without letting it boil, until the gelatin is dissolved, 5 to 10 minutes. Pour into a heatproof cup or small bowl, add the reserved schnapps mixture, and stir together. Blend in the xanthan gum, if using, with an immersion blender.

2. Fill a large bowl with ice cubes and water. Place the cup or bowl in the ice bath until the schnapps mixture is chilled, about 10 minutes.

3. Transfer the gelatin mixture to a whipping siphon and shake. Charge the whipper with one of the N_2O canisters, according to the manufacturer's directions, and shake vigorously. Repeat with the second N_2O canister. Refrigerate for at least an hour and use within three days.

MAKES ENOUGH FOR 10 DRINKS

3 ounces (90 ml) butterscotch schnapps

2 ounces (60 ml) water

6 dashes cardamom bitters

1.1 g 170 bloom–strength gelatin sheet

0.1 g xanthan gum (optional)

2 N_2O chargers

Fats, such
as butter,
are soluble
in ethanol
and can add
a wonderful
richness to
cocktails.

FAT WASHING

Fat washing is a way to infuse spirits with flavor from fats, such as butter, oil, nut butters, or animal fats. The technique works on the principle of polarity: Fat will dissolve in ethanol (aka alcohol) and not in water. It's similar to other infusions in that the alcohol will extract the fat-soluble and water-soluble flavors, but the fat also adds richness to a cocktail. The process typically goes as follows:

1. Melt the fat, if necessary, into a liquid state.

2. Combine it with the alcohol in a wide container to maximize the surface area contact between the two.

3. Let it infuse for a few hours at room temperature.

4. Transfer the container to the freezer to solidify the fats.

5. Strain out the now solid fats through a cheesecloth or coffee filter.

Simply freeze the infusion to solidify the fats then strain them out.

Note: Most fat-washed spirits are shelf stable, but I'd recommend storing them in the fridge to better retain their flavor. If using an animal fat such as bacon, there is a risk of bacteria poisoning. Ensure that all meat fats are fully cooked, store the fat-washed spirit in the fridge, and use it within a few days.

BENTON'S OLD FASHIONED

This drink has become a modern classic and is credited with introducing the concept of fat washing to the world. It was created by Don Lee at the bar Please Don't Tell in Manhattan around 2007. The base is bourbon infused with Benton's bacon, but you can use any thick-cut, hickory-smoked bacon.

MAKES 1 DRINK

2 ounces (60 ml) Bacon-Washed Bourbon (recipe follows)

¼ ounce (7 ml) pure maple syrup

2 dashes Angostura bitters

1 orange twist, for garnish

Half strip of cooked bacon (optional), for garnish

Add a large ice cube (preferably one that's clear; see Clear Ice on page 54) to a chilled rocks glass. Add the bourbon, maple syrup, and bitters and stir to chill and dilute. Squeeze the orange twist to express the essential oils over the drink and drop in the twist. Garnish with the bacon, if desired, and serve.

Bacon-Washed Bourbon

MAKES 750 ML (25 OUNCES)

One 750-ml bottle bourbon

1½ ounces (45 ml) melted fat from fully cooked hickory-smoked bacon (see Note on page 123)

1. Add the bourbon and bacon fat to a large freezer-safe container, stir together, and cover. Let infuse for 4 hours at room temperature. Put in the freezer until the fat solidifies, about 2 hours.

2. Using a small knife, pierce a hole in the layer of fat. Strain the bourbon through a sieve into a large bowl; discard the fat solids. Funnel the bourbon into a 1-quart bottle. Store in the refrigerator and use it within a few days.

In the 19th century, the Old Fashioned was considered a "matutinal" cocktail taken in the morning; adding bacon and maple syrup just makes it a balanced breakfast.

PEANUT BUTTER PATTY (TAGALONG) COCKTAIL

MAKES 1 DRINK

2 ounces (60 ml) Peanut Butter–Infused Bourbon (page 127)

1 barspoon (5 ml) crème de cacao

Dash chocolate bitters

Dash Angostura bitters

½ Peanut Butter Patty (Tagalong), for garnish

I have an unexplainable weakness for peanut butter; it's my guilty food pleasure. My preferred way to consume it is simply jar to mouth, and at any given time there is a shocking number of peanut butter–laden spoons in my dishwasher to prove it. So, when I started experimenting with fat washing, peanut butter was high on my list. One year during Girl Scout cookie season, I finally put the technique to good use in a cocktail inspired by the Tagalong (aka Peanut Butter Patty) cookie. I'm still waiting for the Girl Scouts organization to hire me to tend bar at a ceremony.

Add the bourbon, crème de cacao, and both bitters to a mixing glass with ice. Stir for about 45 seconds. Strain into a chilled rocks glass over a large ice cube (preferably one that's clear; see Clear Ice on page 54). Place the cookie half on top of the ice cube and serve.

COCKTAIL CHEMISTRY

Peanut Butter–Infused Bourbon

1. Spread the peanut butter across the bottom of a 9-by-13-inch baking dish. Pour the bourbon over the top and cover with plastic wrap. Let infuse in the fridge for about 72 hours.

2. Strain the bourbon through a sieve lined with cheesecloth or coffee filters into a large bowl. Funnel the bourbon into a 1-quart bottle. Store in the refrigerator and use within one month.

**MAKES 750 ML
(25 OUNCES)**

16 ounces (150 g) natural unsalted creamy peanut butter

One 750-ml bottle bourbon

FOAMS

A foam is created when gas is dispersed into a liquid, and if done correctly, it can result in a wonderful mouthfeel. The rise of molecular gastronomy led to foams being used in creative ways to add flavors and texture to food and eventually cocktails, and at one point we may have gone overboard on foams. Admittedly, it's a dense topic that could take up multiple chapters, so I'll keep it simple and tailored to the home bartender, with methods for unflavored and flavored foams that use egg whites or gelatin.

EGG WHITE FOAM WITH THE REVERSE DRY SHAKE

If you're just looking to add a richer mouthfeel and frothiness to your cocktail, simply shaking your drink with egg white is the easiest approach. Most sour cocktails benefit from an egg white in my opinion, and it's a staple in classics like the whiskey sour, pisco sour, and the Clover Club. The method I prefer to get a consistently creamy foam is called "the reverse dry shake," which generally goes as follows:

1. Build your cocktail in a shaker glass (or the larger shaker tin).

2. Add ice and shake for 15 seconds.

3. Double strain (pour through a Hawthorne strainer over a fine-mesh strainer) into another vessel or the smaller shaker tin; discard the ice.

4. Add 1 large egg white to the now chilled cocktail and dry shake (without ice) vigorously for 15 seconds.

5. Free pour the cocktail into your glass.

Note: Only use fresh, high-quality eggs in cocktails. Contrary to popular belief, the alcohol will not kill any bacteria such as salmonella, though the risk of getting ill is low. A vegan alternative to 1 large egg white is 1 tablespoon (15 ml) of aquafaba (the liquid from canned chickpeas).

FLAVORED FOAM IN A WHIPPING SIPHON—USING EGG WHITES

Reverse dry shaking with an egg white simply adds a foam to your cocktail, but what if you want the foam to have a different flavor than the cocktail entirely? For this technique I use a whipping siphon (usually a 1-pint [½-liter] iSi whipper) to create the foam. There are several ways to make stable flavored foams ideal for cocktails. The following are the only two methods I use.

If you're looking to create a foam that includes acid, such as lemon juice, I'd stick to egg whites because the acid will help stabilize the egg foam and egg whites are, of course, easy to come by. A general template I follow looks like this:

1. In a bowl, combine 1 ounce (30 ml) of an acid, such as lemon juice, with 1 to 2 ounces (30 to 60 ml) of a sweetener, such as Demerara syrup, and 3 ounces (90 ml) of water to lengthen the foam. Taste the mixture at this point to ensure that it's balanced and adjust the ingredients as necessary.

2. Whisk in 2 large egg whites.

3. Pour everything into your whipping siphon and add an N_2O charger to inject gas into the liquid; shake vigorously.

4. Add a second N_2O charger and shake vigorously again.

5. Refrigerate the siphon for at least an hour to create a more stable foam.

6. Make your cocktail and pour into a glass.

7. Invert the whipping siphon and layer the foam on top.

1. In a liquid measuring cup, combine 3 ounces (90 ml) of a flavored liquid with 2 ounces (60 ml) of water to lengthen the foam. Weigh the mixture.

2. Weigh out 0.75% of that mixture's total liquid weight in 170 bloom-strength gelatin (probably about 1 g).

3. Add half of your liquid mixture to a small saucepan along with the gelatin.

4. Dissolve the gelatin over low heat, then pour in the remaining half of the liquid mixture (the liquid is added in two batches so you don't damage all your flavor with heat).

5. Optionally, weigh out 0.1% of the total liquid weight from the first step in xanthan gum, which will thicken the foam and create a smoother and more durable bubble structure. Blend the xanthan gum into the gelatin mixture with an immersion blender.

6. Chill the gelatin mixture in an ice bath to allow the gelatin to set.

7. Once cooled, pour the mixture into your whipping siphon and add an N_2O charger to inject gas into the liquid, then shake vigorously.

8. Add a second N_2O charger and shake again.

9. Refrigerate the siphon for at least an hour before discharging the foam on top of a cocktail.

FLAVORED FOAM IN A WHIPPING SIPHON—USING GELATIN

Egg white foams can sometimes develop an odor that resembles a wet dog, so alternatively we can use gelatin, which is a colorless and flavorless thickening agent derived from animal collagen. I often use gelatin if my foam doesn't include any acid (such as in Butterscotch Foam, page 121), though the process is a bit more complicated. Here's a template I follow:

INVERTED SAZERAC

The Sazerac is a classic New Orleans cocktail that is a close cousin of the Old Fashioned. It's typically made with rye, Peychaud's bitters, and simple syrup, with an absinthe rinse and lemon twist. What if we amped up the acidity and brought the sweetness into a lightweight foam floated on top of the drink? The result is a beautiful presentation and delicious cocktail that evolves as the foam slowly seeps into the base.

1. Rinse a chilled rocks glass with absinthe and discard what's left in the glass.

2. Add the rye and bitters to a mixing glass with ice and stir for about 45 seconds. Strain into the prepared rocks glass. Layer the foam on top. Squeeze the lemon twist to express the essential oils over the drink, drop in the twist, and serve.

MAKES 1 DRINK

Absinthe, for rinsing

2 ounces (60 ml) rye

3 dashes Peychaud's bitters

Maple Lemon Foam (page 132), for topping

1 lemon twist, for garnish

Maple Lemon Foam

3 ounces (90 ml) water

1½ ounces (45 ml) pure
maple syrup

1 ounce (30 ml) strained
fresh lemon juice

2 large egg whites (see
Note on page 128)

2 N$_2$O chargers

1. Add the water, maple syrup, lemon juice, and egg whites to a small bowl. Beat together briefly with a fork to break up the egg whites and combine the ingredients.

2. Transfer the mixture to a 1-pint (½-liter) whipping siphon (I recommend an iSi whipper). Charge the whipper with one of the N$_2$O canisters, according to the manufacturer's directions, and shake vigorously. Repeat with the second N$_2$O canister. Discharge the second N$_2$O charger to the whipper and shake vigorously. Refrigerate for at least an hour and use within three days.

OLD SPANISH

and other wine cocktails

30 Rock is one of my top three TV comedy series of all time. The density of jokes is off the charts and the acting is world-class. I honestly wish there were more drinks from the show to recreate, but at least the second episode of season seven gave us the amazing Old Spanish cocktail, complete with a full recipe. In this episode, the hapless Cooter Burger (played by Matthew Broderick) lets himself into the office of Jack Donaghy (played by Alec Baldwin) and attempts to make a "cool drink."

The Old Spanish is not a cool drink nor is it a tasty one. In fact, it's not even a real drink as Cooter soon came to learn. But it serves as a good jumping-off point to discuss the use of wine in cocktails.

Side note: The writers over at *Mad Men* did a cheeky nod to their friends at *30 Rock* when the acclaimed TV show's character Ted Chaough orders an Old Spanish in season six.

RECREATED

MAKES 1 DRINK

3 ounces (90 ml) Spanish red wine

3 ounces (90 ml) chilled tonic water

3 Spanish green olives, skewered on a pick, for garnish

Add the wine and tonic to a rocks glass with ice and stir. Garnish with the olives and serve.

IMPROVED OLD SPANISH

MAKES 1 DRINK

3 ounces (90 ml)
amontillado sherry

1 barspoon (5 ml) simple
syrup (page 14)

3 dashes orange bitters

3 ounces (90 ml) chilled
tonic water (I prefer Fever-
Tree)

1 lemon twist, for garnish

Cooter was on track to actually make a pretty tasty beverage with his Old Spanish (page 135) if he didn't ruin it with those olives. Spain loves its wine as well as gin and tonics, so we should be able to find a way for those flavors to come together. To start, let's move from a standard red wine to a fortified wine in some amontillado sherry, which is nutty and rich, allowing it to stand up better to the bitterness of the tonic water. Brighten it up with some orange bitters and a (Liz) lemon twist, and we have a refreshing summer cocktail that's simultaneously savory, sweet, bitter, and acidic.

Add the sherry, simple syrup, and bitters to a Collins glass over ice (preferably a clear ice stick; see Clear Ice on page 54). Pour in the tonic water and stir. Squeeze the lemon twist to express the essential oils over the drink, drop in the twist, and serve with a spoon straw.

I strongly prefer an egg white shaken into my New York Sour.

NEW YORK SOUR

In its most basic form, the New York Sour is just a whiskey sour with a float of red wine. I think of it as the classier cousin of the whiskey sour, and done right, it truly is a drink that's greater than the sum of its parts. The float of wine makes for a beautiful presentation and works due to the principle of specific gravity (see Layering a Cocktail on page 164).

Add the whiskey, lemon juice, simple syrup, and egg white to a shaker tin. Shake for 15 seconds. Add ice and shake for another 15 seconds. Double strain (pour through a Hawthorne strainer over a fine-mesh strainer) into a chilled coupe. Float the wine on top, slowly pouring it over the back of a spoon.

RELATED

MAKES 1 DRINK

2 ounces (60 ml) whiskey

¾ ounce (22 ml) fresh lemon juice

¾ ounce (22 ml) simple syrup (page 14)

1 large egg white

1 ounce (30 ml) dry, full-bodied red wine, like a Malbec, Syrah, or Cabernet Franc

GLÖGG (MULLED WINE)

Heating wine with spices goes back to the ancient Romans, and today there are countless variations of mulled wine from around the world that are often drunk during the winter holiday season. My go-to recipe is a take on Nordic glögg (pronounced "gloog") that includes port and a spirit, such as aquavit or vodka.

---

1. Add the wine, aquavit, port, sugar, cloves, cardamom, cinnamon, nutmeg, and zest to a large pot. Bring to a simmer and let simmer (do not boil), stirring occasionally, for 30 minutes.

2. Remove from the heat and let cool to room temperature, then transfer to a pitcher and refrigerate overnight. Strain through a fine-mesh sieve into a large bowl.

3. To serve, transfer the glögg to a large pot and bring to a simmer (do not boil). Keep warm over low heat and ladle into teacups or other wide-mouth cups. Garnish each cup with a few of the raisins and almonds and serve.

RELATED

MAKES ABOUT TEN 5-OUNCE (150-ML) SERVINGS

2 (750-ml) bottles dry, medium-bodied red wine

5 ounces (150 ml) aquavit or vodka

3 ounces (60 ml) ruby port

1 cup (200 g) Demerara sugar

10 whole cloves

5 whole cardamom pods

5 cinnamon sticks

1 whole nutmeg

Grated zest of 1 orange

¼ cup (40 g) raisins, for garnish

⅓ cup (30 g) slivered almonds, for garnish

SKITTLEBRAU

and other beer cocktails

RECREATED

MAKES 1 DRINK

Handful of Skittles

One 12-ounce can chilled lager beer

Homer is usually a Duff beer kinda guy with the occasional moment of cocktail inspiration (see Flaming Homer, page 169). In episode six of season nine we see that inspiration play out in the Kwik-E-Mart when a lonely Homer asks the owner, Apu, for "that beer that has candy floating in it" called Skittlebrau. Not to be dissuaded by the fact that Skittlebrau doesn't actually exist, Homer settles for a six-pack of beer and a bag of Skittles. I admire the dedication to the idea, wherever it came from, and surprisingly this was one of the tastier recreations I've done.

I guess the Skittlebrau could fall under the umbrella of beer cocktails, which are a pretty niche category of drink; I'm usually in the mood for a beer or a cocktail but rarely both. However, there are a few recipes that have changed my mind about beer cocktails, and I've listed them in this section. If for some reason you want to recreate the Skittlebrau exactly, here's the elusive recipe.

Add the Skittles to a chilled beer glass. Pour the beer into the glass. Stir and taste the rainbow.

IMPROVED SKITTLEBRAU

I love mixing citrus with beer, so when thinking of how to improve the Skittlebrau (page 141), my mind immediately went to a shandy. Shandies go by many names and iterations around the world, but the basic template is beer mixed with a lemon-lime-flavored beverage. For my version, I decided to combine lemon juice and ginger beer with a German hefeweizen (wheat beer) and throw in a few Skittles to pay Homer my respects.

MAKES 1 DRINK

½ ounce (15 ml) fresh lemon juice

A few lemon and lime Skittles

One 12-ounce bottle chilled hefeweizen beer

4 ounces (120 ml) chilled ginger beer

1 lemon wedge, for garnish

Add the lemon juice and Skittles to a chilled beer mug. Pour in the hefeweizen. Top with the ginger beer and stir. Garnish with the lemon wedge and serve.

CERVEZARONI

If you like the Aperol spritz, you'll probably dig this summer sipper. It's like a Mexican take on a Negroni made with beer that I call a Cervezaroni (see what I did there?). I use a light, Mexican pilsner-style beer, but you could swap in an IPA if you're looking for something more hoppy. You can also switch to a different vermouth based on your flavor preferences, but I find the medium-sweet blanc vermouth, rather than a dry vermouth, works best in this template.

MAKES 1 DRINK

½ ounce (15 ml) blanco tequila

1 ounce (30 ml) Campari

½ ounce (15 ml) blanc vermouth

5 ounces Mexican pilsner-style beer (I prefer Pacífico)

Add the tequila, Campari, and vermouth to a chilled Collins glass and stir together. Top with the beer. Add ice and serve.

When making beer cocktails, like the Cervezaroni, always add the ice last to prolong the carbonation.

BITTER EIN BIT

I'll start by saying I'm more proud of this cocktail name than I should be. One of my favorite beers is a German pilsner called Bitburger, which has the slogan "Bitte ein Bit" (translation: "A Bit, please"). So, if we added some bitter amaro and a few other tasty ingredients, what would we call it? Similar to jokes, the best cocktail names are ones you need to explain in detail; you're welcome.

This drink looks a bit like a shandy, however, the addition of Amaro Montenegro adds a wonderful complexity. You can swap in another amaro, but I'd steer clear of intense varieties, such as fernet.

Add the amaro, pineapple juice, lemon juice, and simple syrup to a shaker tin with ice and shake for 15 seconds. Double strain (pour through a Hawthorne strainer over a fine-mesh strainer) into a chilled beer glass. Top with the pilsner. Garnish with the lemon wheel and serve.

MAKES 1 DRINK

1½ ounces (45 ml) Amaro Montenegro

1½ ounces (45 ml) fresh pineapple juice

¾ ounce (22 ml) fresh lemon juice

½ ounce (15 ml) simple syrup (page 14)

Chilled pilsner (ideally Bitburger), for topping

1 lemon wheel, for garnish

A SONG OF ICE AND FIRE

and other ice ball cocktails

The first video on my YouTube channel featured an ice ball cocktail. It's a ridiculous but fun trick that involves creating a spherical ice shell, injecting a cocktail inside that shell, and then smashing it open. I explain how to make the ice ball shell in the next section (see Ice Ball Shell on page 149), but this demo spawned several ice ball experiments—some involving fire, smoke, and color-changing drinks. This Song of Ice and Fire (named after the book series that was later adapted into the TV show *Game of Thrones*) is probably the most insane cocktail I've created. It never actually appears in the series, but at the peak of the show's popularity I wanted to invent a cocktail involving ice and fire. Instead of smashing the shell open here, I skewer the ice ball cocktail to balance it over flaming rum in a martini glass. The flame melts the bottom of the ice ball, slowly releasing the cocktail. Make sure to use a skewer that's long enough to balance the ice ball on the rim of your martini glass.

A note of caution: Always be careful when combining fire and cocktails. Especially for this drink, where a cold cocktail is suddenly introduced to a flaming spirit and there is a risk of thermal shock that could shatter the glass. Only use tempered glasses to make this drink.

recipe continues

continued

MAKES 1 DRINK

Ice Ball Shell (page 149)

⅓ ounce (10 ml) Goslings 151-proof Black Seal rum

1 ounce (30 ml) Goslings 80-proof Black Seal rum

¾ ounce (22 ml) Cointreau

½ ounce (15 ml) fresh lime juice

¼ ounce (7 ml) simple syrup (page 14)

Splash fresh orange juice

Dash orange bitters

1. Using a pointy end of a paper clip, pierce a tiny hole in the ice ball shell a little bit above its equator. Insert a 4.5-inch bamboo skewer in that hole until it reaches the opposite side of the ice ball shell. Pierce another tiny hole in the shell where it meets the end of the skewer and push the skewer through. Balance the skewered ice ball on the rim of a freezer-safe rocks glass. There will probably be a gap in the shell where the skewer emerged, so add a few drops of water to the gap and transfer to the freezer to patch it up.

2. Add the 151-proof rum to a tempered martini glass (see Note on page 147).

3. Combine the 80-proof rum, Cointreau, lime juice, simple syrup, orange juice, and bitters in a shaker tin with ice. Shake until very cold. Using a marinade injector, inject the cocktail into the hole at the top of your prepared ice ball shell until it fills the shell completely.

4. Carefully ignite the 151-proof rum. Holding the ends of the skewer, carefully transfer the ice ball cocktail to the martini glass, centering it over the flame and balancing the skewer on the rim of the glass. The flame will slowly start to melt the bottom of the ice ball, allowing the cocktail to pour out and extinguish the flame. Remove the shell to sip the cocktail.

ICE BALL SHELL

This technique is really what launched my YouTube channel. My very first video was "How to Make an Ice Ball Cocktail" and it went viral. I was inspired by a drink called the Old Fashioned in the Rocks at the innovative Aviary bar in Chicago, where they use a blast chiller to freeze water balloons at super-cold temperatures to create a hollow ice shell for an Old Fashioned. My challenge was to adapt this technique to the home bartender without requiring expensive tools.

All you need is a standard 2.5-inch ice ball mold, a marinade injector, and the ability to keep track of time. Here's the trick: When you put the ice ball mold in the freezer, it freezes the water from the outside in. So, if you unmold the ice ball before it freezes all the way through, you can drain the unfrozen water inside the ice shell, then store the shell in the freezer until you're ready to inject a cocktail into it.

But how to drink the cocktail? Some people like to insert a straw in the hole where the water was drained from the ice ball shell, others like to smash the shell open (carefully!) with a spoon or small hammer. Or you can replicate the Aviary method and slingshot a weight (like a hex nut) threaded through a rubber band over the top of the glass to smash the shell.

You need to ensure the ice shell is sufficiently thick so that it doesn't instantly leak when a cocktail is introduced, but not too thick to hamper smashing or to reduce its capacity to hold a cocktail. The shell thickness is largely determined by the temperature of your freezer and how long you freeze the ice ball, so you may have to experiment to get it right. For my -6°F (-21°C) freezer, about 3 hours (flipping the ice mold halfway through) results in the perfect shell. This holds about 3 ounces (90 ml) of cocktail inside.

The ice ball freezes from the outside in, so removing it from the freezer before it freezes all the way through will result in an ice shell with water inside.

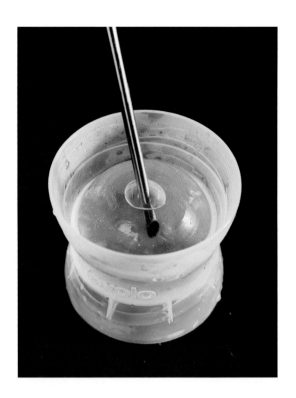

HERE ARE THE STEP-BY-STEP INSTRUCTIONS:

1. Fill a 2.5-inch ice ball mold with cold filtered water and place in the freezer for 3 hours, flipping it halfway through. This helps freeze the shell into an even thickness all the way around.

2. Remove the ice mold from the freezer and let sit at room temperature for a few minutes to temper, then open up the mold.

3. Heat the tip of your marinade injector with hot water and puncture a hole in the top of the ice shell.

4. Using the marinade injector, suction all the water from the ice ball shell, then discard the water.

5. Remove the shell from the mold and place it hole-side up in a freezer-safe airtight container.

6. Cover and freeze until ready to use. (This will result in a small, flat base forming at the bottom of the shell).

7. When ready to use, transfer the ice ball shell to a rocks glass. Let sit at room temperature for at least 5 minutes to temper.

COLOR-CHANGING OLD SMASHIONED

RELATED

About two years after debuting my ice ball cocktail, I finally gave the method a proper name: the Old Smashioned. This recipe is another fun way to apply the technique, using color-shifting butterfly pea flower tea. This tea is a deep blue color, but it also acts as a pH indicator, turning to purple when mixed with an acid, such as citrus juice. Smash the ice ball open to release the tea and some gin and watch the drink change color as it meets the lemon juice in the glass.

MAKES 1 DRINK

2 ounces (60 ml) gin

1 ounce (30 ml) fresh brewed butterfly pea flower tea, chilled

Ice Ball Shell (page 150)

¾ ounce (22 ml) fresh lemon juice

¾ ounce (22 ml) simple syrup (page 14)

1. Add 1 ounce (30 ml) of the gin and the tea to a mixing glass with ice and stir together. Using a marinade injector, inject this blue liquid into the hole at the top of the ice ball shell until it fills the shell completely, then place it in a rocks glass.

2. Add the lemon juice, simple syrup, and remaining gin to the mixing glass. Stir with ice until chilled. Pour around the ice ball. Thread a rubber band through a hex nut and hold it taut with your thumb and index finger over the rocks glass. Pull the nut with your other hand to create a slingshot, then release the nut to smash open the ice ball. Stir until the blue tea reacts with the lemon juice to turn purple.

RELATED

MAKES 1 DRINK

1 ounce (30 ml) mezcal

1 ounce (30 ml) Campari

1 ounce (30 ml) sweet vermouth

Ice Ball Shell (page 150)

Pinch of applewood chips

FOG BURNER

My YouTube channel was born in San Francisco, where the fog is such a fixture of the city that it even has a name: Karl. On most days, the morning fog is burned away by the afternoon sun, which inspired my Fog Burner cocktail. In short, it's a mezcal Negroni served inside a hollow ice ball and presented under a smoke-filled glass. The visual effect is stunning, and the applewood smoke nicely complements the smoky mezcal.

For the presentation, I like to balance the ice ball on a chilled jigger, which is placed inside a small bowl to catch any spillover. I use a smoking gun to blast applewood smoke into a stemless wineglass, which I then invert over the top of the ice ball, effectively hiding the ice ball in the smoke. This makes the reveal all the more glorious when you lift the glass and waft away the smoke to reveal the bright red orb. It's best to serve this with a small straw instead of smashing the shell.

1. Add the mezcal, Campari, and vermouth to a mixing glass. Stir briskly with ice for about 45 seconds.

2. Using a marinade injector, inject the cocktail into the hole at the top of the ice ball shell until it fills the shell completely and place on a chilled jigger in a bowl.

3. Add the wood chips to a smoking gun and ignite them according to the manufacturer's directions. Using the smoking gun, fill a stemless wineglass or glass cloche with smoke and invert over the prepared ice ball, trapping the smoke around it. To serve the cocktail, lift up the smoke-filled glass and insert a short straw in the hole at the top of the ice ball.

PEPPERMINT PATTY

and other hot chocolate cocktails

When I was a kid, I had strict limits on how much sugar I was allowed to consume each day, which, of course, led to me having a raging sweet tooth as an adult. So, my reaction to a sweet and boozy hot chocolate is very similar to secret agent Archer's reaction to trying his Peppermint Patty creation: "OH MY GOD." Good thing these are seasonal.

In season six, episode three of the eponymous TV series, Archer is en route to a mountain climbing resort in the Alps to kill an assassin when he invents this minty hot cocoa. I always assumed mint and chocolate were a classic combination, but based on the comments from my YouTube video, uniting those flavors is quite polarizing. I'm on team mint chocolate, and the two flavors are great together in this recipe.

RECREATED

MAKES 1 DRINK

6 ounces (180 ml) whole milk

2 tablespoons (15 g) sweetened dark hot cocoa mix

1 ounce (30 ml) peppermint schnapps

½ ounce (15 ml) crème de cacao

1 barspoon (5 ml) crème de menthe

Combine the milk and cocoa mix in a small saucepan, stir, and bring to a boil. Immediately remove from the heat and pour into a Styrofoam cup. Add the schnapps, crème de cacao, and crème de menthe. Stir together and serve.

RELATED

RUM HOT COCOA

MAKES 1 DRINK

1 cup (235 ml) whole milk

2 tablespoons (16 g) unsweetened Dutch-processed cocoa powder

1½ tablespoons (18 g) sugar

Pinch of salt

1½ ounces (45 ml) dark rum

¼ ounce (7 ml) crème de menthe

2 marshmallows, skewered on a cocktail pick, for garnish

If you want to step up your cocoa game, I highly recommend using unsweetened Dutch-processed cocoa instead of a cocoa mix that's already sweetened. You'll immediately notice a richer chocolate flavor and you can sweeten it to your liking. This comes in handy when mixing in other ingredients that are already sweetened, such as liqueurs (like crème de menthe).

Dark rum is an excellent spirit to pair with hot cocoa, and in this recipe I wanted just a hint of mint, much more subtle than in the Peppermint Patty (page 155).

Add the milk, cocoa powder, sugar, and salt to a small saucepan and bring to a simmer, whisking to combine. Pour the hot cocoa into a mug. Add the rum and crème de menthe and stir. Garnish with the marshmallows and brown them with a culinary torch, then serve.

SPIKED MEXICAN HOT CHOCOLATE

RELATED

Mexican table chocolate is a sweetened chocolate that's spiced with cinnamon. It often comes in a hockey puck–shaped tablet; has a rough, gritty texture; and is primarily used for making hot chocolate. And what a fine cup of chocolate it makes. I mix this with a nice reposado tequila and a little Ancho Reyes chile liqueur for a mild kick. It's just wonderful.

MAKES 1 DRINK

1 cup (235 ml) whole milk

¼ tablet (23 g) Mexican table chocolate (such as Ibarra)

1 ounce (30 ml) reposado tequila

1 ounce (30 ml) Ancho Reyes chile liqueur

4 ounces (120 ml) heavy whipping cream

Freshly grated cinnamon stick, for garnish

1. Combine the milk and chocolate in a small saucepan and warm over low heat until the chocolate is melted. Pour the hot chocolate into a warmed Irish coffee mug. Add the tequila and Ancho Reyes and stir.

2. Add the cream to a shaker tin and shake until thickened, about 1 minute. Float the whipped cream on top of the hot chocolate, slowly pouring it over the back of a spoon. Grate cinnamon over the drink and serve.

WHIPPING CREAM IN A COCKTAIL SHAKER

When you're making an Irish Coffee (page 102), hot cocoa, or any other drink that calls for whipped cream, I highly recommend whipping your own. This allows you to whip it to your desired consistency or sweeten it to your liking (I prefer it unsweetened).

You can use a handheld mixer, whipping siphon, or any number of tools to whip air into cream. But if you're making a cocktail, chances are you have a shaker tin on hand that does the trick. Simply add your designated amount of heavy whipping cream to the tin (no more than halfway full at a time), cover it, and shake vigorously until the cream reaches your desired consistency. It usually takes me about 60 seconds to get the cream to the point where I can free pour it over the drink and it will float on top. Pour it over the back of a spoon to get a clean layer.

For cocktails, whipped cream should be thin enough to pour freely from the tin, but thick enough to still sit on top of the drink. Pouring it over the back of a spoon helps achieve that clean layer on top.

CHARTREUSE HOT CHOCOLATE

MAKES 1 DRINK

1 cup (235 ml) whole milk

1 tablespoon (8 g) unsweetened Dutch-processed cocoa powder

Pinch of salt

2 ounces (55 g) chopped semisweet chocolate, plus more to shave for garnish

1½ ounces (45 ml) Green Chartreuse

4 ounces (120 ml) heavy whipping cream

The herbal liqueur Green Chartreuse is one of my favorite cocktail ingredients of all time, and it happens to pair very well with hot chocolate. Because Green Chartreuse is already quite sweet I don't add any sugar to this recipe, but I do use semisweet chocolate in addition to cocoa powder to really dial the richness up to eleven. This is truly the only hot chocolate I need in my life. Make it and thank me later.

1. Combine the milk, cocoa powder, and salt in a small saucepan. Whisk in the chopped chocolate and warm over medium heat until the chocolate is melted. Pour the hot chocolate into a warmed Irish coffee mug. Add the Green Chartreuse and stir.

2. Add the cream to a shaker tin and shake until thickened, about 1 minute. Float the whipped cream on top of the hot cocoa, slowly pouring it over the back of a spoon. Shave some semisweet chocolate over the whipped cream and serve.

INFINITY COCKTAIL
and other layered cocktails

RECREATED

MAKES 1 SWEET MESS OF A DRINK

½ ounce (15 ml) grenadine

½ ounce (15 ml) blue Curaçao

½ ounce (15 ml) crème de violette

½ ounce (15 ml) Yellow Chartreuse

½ ounce (15 ml) Grand Marnier

½ ounce (15 ml) Green Chartreuse

The infinity stones play a central role in Marvel comics and film, especially the Avengers series. Created during the Big Bang, these gemlike objects grant whoever wields them various powers related to their aspect of existence, such as time and space. The villain Thanos sought to collect all six stones (Mind, Power, Reality, Soul, Space, and Time), which would render him a godlike being to control the universe.

So, when the movie *Avengers: Endgame* was released, I decided to create a rainbow-striped cocktail that uses six different liqueurs, each representing a different color infinity stone: grenadine for the red Reality stone, blue Curaçao for the blue Space stone, crème de violette for the purple Power stone, Yellow Chartreuse for the yellow Mind stone, Grand Marnier for the orange Soul stone, and Green Chartreuse for the green Time stone. I modeled the Infinity Cocktail after a notorious type of drink called the pousse-café, a concoction of layered liqueurs so labor-intensive that ordering one might get you kicked out of the bar. Though ill-advised, making the Infinity Cocktail provided an opportunity to discuss the concept of specific gravity and how layered cocktails work (see Layering a Cocktail on page 164).

Ironically, for someone like Thanos who is obsessed with "balancing" the universe, this is a decidedly unbalanced cocktail. Like the pousse-café, the Infinity Cocktail is mostly a stack of sweet liqueurs that is literally just the sum of its parts, nothing greater.

Add the grenadine to a Champagne flute. Then using a cocktail layering tool or the back of a spoon, slowly pour each successive liqueur in the order listed to keep each colored layer distinct, rinsing the layering tool or spoon with water after each layer.

LAYERING
A COCKTAIL

The key to creating those striking layers in a cocktail is stacking each liquid in order of decreasing density to keep each layer distinct. The density of a liquid is influenced by a variety of factors, including the sugar and ethanol content. Normally you don't have to think about this when building cocktails, but it certainly comes into play when trying to create a layered or floated effect. To understand if one liquid will float on top of another liquid, we need to consider the relative density of the liquids, also known as the specific gravity. Drinks like the New York Sour (page 1139) rely on this concept to achieve its signature float of red wine on top.

The specific gravity of a liquid can actually be quantified, often as the ratio of its density to that of water (water itself has a specific gravity of 1). The higher the specific gravity, the more dense the liquid, meaning it should be poured into the glass first as it will sink to the bottom.

All things being equal, higher ethanol content will result in a lower specific gravity (since ethanol is less dense than water), and higher sugar concentration will result in a higher specific gravity.

There are charts online that try to calculate the specific gravity of various spirits and liqueurs, which can be helpful when building layered cocktails, or you can just experiment the old-fashioned way.

The most common technique for layering is to slowly pour each liquid over the back of a spoon, but you can make the lines even cleaner by using a professional cocktail layering tool. Be sure to rinse the spoon or layering tool after each layer for the most striking effect.

This layering tool has a little buoy that floats on top of the drink and slowly allows liquid to pour onto the surface of the drink.

SAMARIAN SUNSET

MAKES 1 DRINK

½ **ounce (15 ml) Campari**

2 **ounces (60 ml) blanco tequila**

¾ **ounce (22 ml) fresh lime juice**

½ **ounce (15 ml) fresh orange juice**

½ **ounce (15 ml) simple syrup (page 14)**

1 **maraschino cherry, for garnish (I typically use Luxardo brand)**

When writing about layered cocktails, I felt compelled to include a recipe for the classic Tequila Sunrise but ended up stumbling upon a delicious variation on this dark ages cocktail called the Samarian Sunset. Created by New York City bartender Natasha David, this drink swaps out grenadine for Campari and adds lime and simple syrup for balance. It's excellent, and though still beautifully layered, the presentation falls far short of the fictional Samarian Sunset from *Star Trek*, which turned from clear to a swirl of orange and gold luminescence when the rim of the glass was tapped sharply. One day I'll figure out how to do that.

1. Pour the Campari into a chilled rocks glass and add a large ice cube (preferably one that's clear; see Clear Ice on page 54).

2. Add the tequila, lime juice, orange juice, and simple syrup to a shaker tin with ice. Shake and carefully strain over the center of the large ice cube in the rocks glass so the drink floats over the Campari. Place the cherry in the divot that has now formed on the top of the ice cube and serve.

FLAMING HOMER
and other flaming cocktails

RECREATED

This was the first cocktail I made that was inspired by a TV show or movie, trying to recreate exactly what appeared on-screen and then seeing if I could improve it. By the sheer number of *Simpsons* cocktails in this book you can tell I'm a fan of the show, and at first glance this iconic cocktail was a great one to kick off my recreations. I was wrong, and you'll see why shortly.

But let's set the scene first. In season three, episode ten, Homer finds himself stuck watching a boring slideshow of his in-laws' vacation photos and desperately needs a drink. Realizing that he is out of beer, he hastily mixes the remains of every liquor bottle in the cabinet, plus a little cough syrup that would later prove to be the game-changing ingredient in this concoction. Homer takes a sip; it doesn't make him go blind, so it'll do. But back on the couch, a stray ash from a cigarette lights the drink on fire and magically turns it into a delicious beverage. Hilarity ensues in a classic *Simpsons* episode.

In retrospect, this was not an ideal drink to remake since we don't really know exactly what went into the original. I did a frame-by-frame analysis of the bottles and recreated the drink solely based on what we knew Homer poured into the blender, including some purple cough syrup. In the end, it was nasty and didn't ignite a mushroom cloud of fire into the air like in the show. Hell, it didn't even catch on fire because the ingredients' proof wasn't high enough (learn more about this in Flaming Lime Boat on page 172).

Note: Don't actually make this drink or ever consume cough syrup with your alcohol.

MAKES 1 TERRIBLE, NONFLAMMABLE DRINK

4 ounces (120 ml) reposado tequila

4 ounces (120 ml) crème de menthe

4 ounces (120 ml) peppermint schnapps

2 ounces (60 ml) children's grape-flavored cough syrup

Add the tequila, crème de menthe, schnapps, and cough syrup to a blender. Blend until combined. Pour into a glass. Try (and fail) to light it on fire.

RELATED

MAKES 1 DRINK

¾ ounce (22 ml) crème de violette

¾ ounce (22 ml) Cointreau

¾ ounce (22 ml) gin

¾ ounce (22 ml) fresh lime juice, plus a completely reamed out lime half for the lime boat

2 teaspoons (10 ml) high-proof spirit (at least 151 proof) or lemon extract

IMPROVED FLAMING HOMER

After the first attempt at recreating the Flaming Homer (page 169), I decided that it needed a complete overhaul so it can actually be palatable. First, how about we not use cough syrup? Can we all agree to that? We're not making "lean," or "purple drank," here; we're keeping it classy.

To get the purple color I grabbed a bottle of crème de violette, a liqueur flavored with violets that's a key ingredient in the Aviation cocktail. The flame component can be tricky—we want something with a proof high enough to ignite for a theatrical presentation, but which still renders the drink tasty. So, I went with a flaming lime boat, which is a fun trick borrowed from tiki cocktails. You basically ignite a high-proof alcohol in a hollowed-out lime half and float that in the drink, saving you from having to consume the lit alcohol. To learn more about this technique and how to achieve the brightest flame, see Flaming Lime Boat on page 172.

1. Add the crème de violette, Cointreau, gin, and lime juice to a shaker tin with ice and shake for 15 seconds. Double strain (pour through a Hawthorne strainer over a fine-mesh strainer) into a chilled coupe.

2. Use your spent lime half as a little boat and float it on the surface of the drink. Add your high-proof spirit or lemon extract to the lime boat, ignite it with a lighter or long match (see Note regarding fire safety on page 172), and serve. Extinguish the flame and remove the lime boat before drinking (do not pour the high-proof spirit or lemon extract into the drink).

FLAMING LIME BOAT

Note: First things first, any technique involving fire should be taken extremely seriously and only utilized if you take the proper safety precautions. Don't prepare near highly flammable materials and always have a plan for putting out a flame, such as having a fire extinguisher nearby.

When done safely, a bit of fire or sparks in your drink can surprise and delight your guests. But what's the best way to incorporate it? First, let's understand how alcohol proof and temperature play a role here. The term "proof" is actually quite relevant to this topic; it dates back to sixteenth-century England when spirits were taxed based on their alcohol content, and so spirits were often given a "burn-or-no-burn" test. If it ignited, it was "above proof" and if not, then "under proof." That cutoff point was set at 100 proof (50% ABV or alcohol by volume) and became the basis for taxation.

But it's not just the alcohol by volume that determines whether or not the liquid will burn; the starting temperature of the liquid plays a material part as well. For example, a 70% ABV spirit will ignite with a flame when it reaches at least 70°F (21°C). This threshold temperature is referred to as the "flash point." Compare that to a 20% ABV liqueur, which has a drastically higher flash point of 97°F (36°C).

Now that we know we can flame a spirit, how can we up the ante? Igniting your booze will often result in a disappointing looking blue flame, but there's a sneaky trick to getting those bright yellow flames you see in tiki cocktails. The secret? Lemon extract, and there are three reasons why you should use it. First, it has a high ABV (upward of 85%). Second, it contains a good amount of oils from lemon peel, which create that bright yellow flame. Third, it's food safe (though I wouldn't recommend consuming it). The downside is that it can be pricier (per ounce) than a cheap high-proof spirit.

Okay, so you want to make a flaming lime boat. Here are the steps I typically follow:

1. Using a citrus reamer, remove the pulp from half a lime. The drier you can make the interior, the better.

2. This is optional, but I often add a "wick," such as a sugar cube or an airy cube of bread, to the lime boat.

3. Add a healthy pour of lemon extract (or a spirit that's at least 151 proof), about 2 teaspoons (10 ml), to the lime boat and douse the "wick," if you're using one.

4. Float the boat on the surface of the drink.

5. Ignite the "wick" or lemon extract directly with a lighter or long match.

6. For some fun sparks, hit the flame with a pinch of cinnamon or cocoa powder.

FLAMING COCKTAILS   **173**

FLAMING A CITRUS PEEL

You don't need to buy extracts to ignite citrus oils—the flammable oils live right within the citrus peels. Bartenders often take advantage of this trick to flame a citrus peel, creating a dramatic swoosh of fire over a drink. If you slice a bit of orange peel and take a close look, you'll notice little pores on the surface that contain essential oils that get expressed when squeezed. Over 90 percent of the oils found in orange and lemon peels is made up of limonene, which gives citrus fruit its familiar aroma and is used in perfumes and household cleaners. This also makes a citrus twist a popular garnish for cocktails, as those fragrant oils can brighten up the drink.

But that limonene is also highly flammable, resulting in a bright yellow fireball when you express those oils over a lighter or match. Now some folks claim this technique will "caramelize" the oils, or impart some unique flavor to the drink. I have no idea where this notion came from, but there is no sugar in citrus oils to caramelize. This trick is all about the visual effect.

To get the best results from this technique, I usually go with an orange since it has more oils in the zest. It's also important to use fresh citrus with a thick peel to ensure the oils haven't dried out.

Here are the steps to flaming a citrus peel (see photo on page 61):

1. From an orange or a lemon, cut an oval-shaped disk of peel with some pith but no flesh.

2. Hold the peel with your index and middle fingers at one end, your thumb at the other.

3. Angle the peel over your glass about 2 inches from the surface.

4. Bring a lighter or lit match in between the drink and the peel and warm the surface of the peel for a few seconds to loosen the oils.

5. Squeeze the peel quickly so that it folds in half and rapidly expels the oils through the flame and over the drink.

6. Discard the peel or drop it in the drink.

WILDFIRE

I created this drink to celebrate the final season of the show *Game of Thrones*, which turned out to be an utter disappointment. But the drink was quite excellent, referencing the pyromancer's bright green concoction that burns so hot it can melt steel. A great weapon for battle, so let's drink it!

For this cocktail, I take advantage of some of the concepts we learned earlier in this section, including the required ABV (alcohol by volume) to ignite a spirit and how cocoa powder can create theatrical sparks when thrown over a flame.

For our green flammable liquid, I use Green Chartreuse, which clocks in at 55% ABV, ignite it in a glass, stoke the flame with a sprinkle of cocoa powder, then build the remaining ingredients in the glass. As we learned in my Chartreuse Hot Chocolate recipe (page 160), chocolate happens to pair very well with Green Chartreuse.

MAKES 1 DRINK

1 ounce (30 ml) Green Chartreuse

Pinch of unsweetened cocoa powder

¼ ounce (7 ml) mezcal (at least 45% ABV)

¼ ounce (7 ml) fresh lime juice

Add the Green Chartreuse to a tempered Nick & Nora glass and ignite with a lighter or long match (see Notes on page 147 and 172). Swirl to build the flame and dash with the cocoa powder to create sparks. Slowly add the mezcal and lime juice to avoid dousing the flame, then add a cube of ice to extinguish it completely and serve.

BABY YODA COCKTAIL

and other last word variations

The Mandalorian is a space western series in the Star Wars franchise that debuted in 2019 and follows a bounty hunter on the lam after being sent to retrieve "the Child." This little creature is of the same species as Yoda, and the world collectively became obsessed with "Baby Yoda." Baby Yoda memes spread like wildfire, knockoff merch sold on the black market, and even cocktail culture couldn't escape the trend.

The so-called Baby Yoda cocktail that made the internet rounds was in fact just a cute and clever way to dress up a coupe glass like Baby Yoda, and it was first created at the Laka Lono Rum Club in Nebraska. The only requirement for the beverage is, of course, that it be green, so for my version I went with the Last Word, arguably the greatest equal parts cocktail ever created (Negroni fans, calm down). I dubbed this "Baby Yoda's First Word," and after we make this adorable drink I'll explore some of my favorite variations on the Last Word template.

1. Drape the napkin around the stem of a chilled coupe and secure with the twine to create Baby Yoda's robe.

2. Add the gin, Chartreuse, maraschino liqueur, and lime juice to a shaker tin with ice. Shake for 15 seconds. Double strain (pour through a Hawthorne strainer over a fine-mesh strainer) into the prepared glass. Cut a slit in the rind of each lime wedge and prop them slit side down on the rim of the glass to create Baby Yoda's ears. Balance the cocktail pick on the rim of the glass, lining up the cherries to create the eyes. Serve.

RECREATED

1 DRINK, THIS MAKES

1 brown paper napkin or square of burlap

A 6-inch (150-mm) length of twine

¾ ounce (22 ml) London dry gin

¾ ounce (22 ml) Green Chartreuse

¾ ounce (22 ml) maraschino liqueur

¾ ounce (22 ml) fresh lime juice

2 lime wedges, each ¼ inch (6 mm) wide at the rind, for garnish

2 dark-colored maraschino cherries (not the bright red variety; I typically use Luxardo brand), skewered on a cocktail pick long enough to balance on the rim of a coupe, for garnish

THE FINAL WARD

MAKES 1 DRINK

¾ **ounce (22 ml) rye**

¾ **ounce (22 ml) Green Chartreuse**

¾ **ounce (22 ml) maraschino liqueur**

¾ **ounce (22 ml) fresh lemon juice**

The Final Ward was created by Phil Ward during his tenure at the legendary New York City bar Death & Co, but it was derived from his "Mr. Potato Head" theory on making cocktails: Every cocktail template (like the one for the Last Word) is simply a blueprint for other good drinks.

For me, this has proven absolutely true, and the idea was taken a step further in the book *Cocktail Codex*, authored by fellow Death & Co alums Alex Day and David Kaplan, along with writer Nick Fauchald. Their thesis is that there are only six foundational cocktails, each with a standard template that can spawn many variations. It's a masterpiece of a book and should be on your shelf next to this one.

But back to the Final Ward. Phil swaps out the gin in the Last Word for rye, which tends to pair better with lemon than lime, so he does a citrus swap as well. It's a wonderfully balanced drink and one of my favorites.

Add the rye, Chartreuse, maraschino liqueur, and lemon juice to a shaker tin with ice. Shake for 15 seconds. Double strain (pour through a Hawthorne strainer over a fine-mesh strainer) into a chilled coupe and serve.

LAST OF THE OAXACANS

RELATED

Probably my favorite of the Last Word variations, this one simply swaps mezcal for the gin. Oaxaca in southwestern Mexico is the capital of mezcal production and where most of the world's mezcal originates, and I do love a clever cocktail name. Here's a pro tip: If you like mezcal, try swapping this smoky agave spirit for the gin in any cocktail. Most ingredients that pair well with gin happen to pair well with mezcal, including those in the Negroni, one of my go-to gin and mezcal swaps.

Add the mezcal, Chartreuse, maraschino liqueur, and lime juice to a shaker tin with ice. Shake for 15 seconds. Double strain (pour through a Hawthorne strainer over a fine-mesh strainer) into a chilled coupe and serve.

MAKES 1 DRINK

¾ ounce (22 ml) mezcal

¾ ounce (22 ml) Green Chartreuse

¾ ounce (22 ml) maraschino liqueur

¾ ounce (22 ml) fresh lime juice

INDUSTRY SOUR

MAKES 1 DRINK

1 ounce (30 ml) Fernet-Branca

1 ounce (30 ml) Green Chartreuse

1 ounce (30 ml) fresh lime juice

1 ounce (30 ml) simple syrup (page 14)

This drink is intense. It was designed by bartender Ted Kilgore in 2011 for industry professionals, as it includes two potent ingredients that bartenders tend to love: Green Chartreuse and fernet. A seemingly dangerous combination, as both spirits have strong herbal notes and can turn off novice cocktail drinkers. My initial intrigue for this drink quickly turned to concern when I first poured it out of the shaker tin; with its dark orange and brownish color, it's one of the ugliest cocktails I've seen. But, hot damn, if it isn't tasty. If you like fernet and Green Chartreuse, make this immediately. If you are on the fence, make it anyway. Just don't bother snapping a photo.

Add the fernet, Chartreuse, lime juice, and simple syrup to a shaker tin with ice. Shake for 15 seconds. Double strain (pour through a Hawthorne strainer over a fine-mesh strainer) into a chilled coupe. Close your eyes and sip.

WAKE-UP JUICE

and other breakfast cocktails

Great Scott! In the third installment of the *Back to the Future* movie franchise, the absent-minded scientist (and DeLorean enthusiast) Doc Brown is transported back in time to the year 1885. He finds himself in love with a local nineteenth-century dame who spurns his advances, refusing to believe he is from the future. As we've all done in this situation, Doc hits the saloon aiming to binge drink away his sorrows, but after one shot of whiskey he passes out. His buddy and time-traveling partner, Marty McFly, arrives on the scene and needs to revive him fast, so the bartender calls for an order of "wake-up juice" that'll make him "as sober as a priest on Sunday."

After the bartender pours a bunch of powders and red sauces into a beer glass and Marty literally funnels the sludge down Doc's unconscious throat, Doc jolts up screaming at the top of his lungs. So, you can imagine how excited I was to re-create and taste this on my YouTube channel.

I was able to identify the exact ingredients in this rousing beverage by locating the original movie script, and I'm happy to share the recipe with you—but, please, don't make wake-up juice. This was, however, a great opportunity to explore some other drinks designed for a groggy Sunday morning. Make those instead.

RECREATED

MAKES ENOUGH FOR 1 FUNNEL

4 ounces (120 ml) pickled jalapeño brine

3 ounces (90 ml) white vinegar

One 2-ounce (60-ml) bottle Tabasco sauce

4 tablespoons (45 g) mustard seeds

3 tablespoons (18 g) onion powder

Few dashes cayenne pepper

Combine all of the ingredients in a beer mug and stir together. Plug nose and drink with a funnel—but, really, do not attempt to drink this.

RELATED

BLOODY MARY

MAKES 1 DRINK

4 ounces (120 ml) tomato juice

2 ounces (60 ml) vodka

½ ounce (15 ml) fresh lemon juice

¼ ounce (7 ml) Worcestershire sauce

½ barspoon (3 ml) prepared horseradish, or to taste

2 dashes Tabasco, or to taste

Celery stick, for garnish

Salt and freshly ground pepper

Your choice of pickled vegetables, skewered on a cocktail pick, for garnish

In my view, the Bloody Mary is less of a hangover "cure" than a well-disguised excuse to get a nice buzz on at 10 a.m. I mean, look how we dress these things—at its most tame the Bloody Mary resembles a nutrient-packed juice shake. At its most extreme, it's a whole damn meal precariously skewered into the glass.

Bloody Mary embellishments can be ridiculous and fun, and I love that there are an infinite number of ways to play with the ingredients and garnishes. Here I'll just share my most basic template for the drink, but feel free to bust open your spice cabinet and have at it.

- **PRO TIP 1:** Don't overdilute your Bloody Mary. Instead, give it a gentle shake or stir with ice and serve over a large ice stick or cube.

- **PRO TIP 2:** To convert your Bloody Mary into the Canadian favorite Bloody Caesar cocktail, swap the base of tomato juice for Clamato, which is a surprisingly delicious bottled mix of tomato juice and clam broth.

- **PRO TIP 3:** For a Mexican-inspired spin with more complexity, swap the vodka with tequila to create a Bloody Maria.

Add the tomato juice, vodka, lemon juice, Worcestershire, horseradish, and Tabasco to a shaker tin with ice and gently shake for 5 seconds. Strain into a chilled double rocks glass over a large ice cube. Garnish with the celery stick, salt and pepper, and pickled vegetables and serve.

GORDON'S BREAKFAST

The best breakfast cocktail I've ever had is a riff on the Gordon's Cup from the late Sasha Petraske, who founded the legendary Milk & Honey bar in New York City. Called Gordon's Breakfast, it's a sloppy mess of fresh and savory ingredients, as any good morning cocktail should be. It involves some heavy muddling action of both lime wedges and cucumber slices and specifically calls for Cholula hot sauce, which I highly recommend using, though you could swap in your favorite brand in a pinch.

The only downside of this drink is that it is rather labor intensive with all the muddling, making it hard to batch and scale to large groups. I'd caution against signing up to make these at a brunch party or you'll never leave the bar.

Combine the gin, simple syrup, Cholula, and Worcestershire in a shaker tin. Add the cucumber and lime. Muddle to extract the lime and cucumber juices. Add 8 cracked ice cubes and shake for 6 seconds. Free pour into a chilled double rocks glass. Garnish with the salt and pepper and serve.

RELATED

MAKES 1 DRINK

2 ounces (60 ml) gin

¾ ounce (22 ml) simple syrup (page 14)

1 barspoon (5 ml) Cholula hot sauce

½ barspoon (3 ml) Worcestershire sauce

4 cucumber wheels

6 lime wedges, each ½ inch wide at the rind

Pinch each of kosher salt and freshly ground pepper, for garnish

ACKNOWLEDGMENTS

TO MY PARTNER, RISHITA: *Cocktail Chemistry* simply wouldn't be possible without your incredible support. Thank you for being my biggest cheerleader. You encouraged me to keep going when the last thing I wanted to do is another voice-over for the YouTube channel. Most important, you let me take over the kitchen cupboards with my ridiculous collection of cocktail gear and glassware!

TO MY SISTER, ALI: Your guidance on navigating the publishing process was beyond helpful. You will always be the truly creative one in the family.

TO MY PARENTS, JUDE AND STEVE: Your unwavering support of my career and the journey of Cocktail Chemistry is one of the greatest gifts I'll ever receive, and I thank you from the bottom of my heart.

TO MY DAUGHTER, DEVIN: You're just fifteen months old at the time of writing this book and the only person I encourage to drink straight from the bottle. I hope you remain a curious little weirdo forever.

TO MY FRIENDS DAVID LERMAN AND CINDY SONG: Thank you for being my unofficial consultants on everything from content ideas to feedback. You have been genuinely invested in the growth of Cocktail Chemistry, and I appreciate it more than you know.

TO MY AGENT TEAM, KIM WITHERSPOON AND JESSICA MILEO: You were my spirit guides for my first book. Thank you for handling every little thing with such confidence and composure.

TO MY EDITOR, JUSTIN SCHWARTZ: Your guidance and partnership in bringing this book to life has been nothing short of amazing. Thank you for taking a chance on me and for having patience with all my (often last-minute) changes or ideas. I'm so proud of what we created.

TO MY PHOTOGRAPHER, AUBRIE PICK: You're an absolute rock star and genuinely wonderful human. Thank you for all your creative energy during your first shoot as a new mom, and for teaching me how to "relax the hand" when holding a cocktail glass.

TO MY CO-WRITER, SUSAN CHOUNG: Thank you for going above and beyond in your research, fact-checking, and creative suggestions. Having you along for the ride was invaluable.

TO YOU: Thank you for supporting my weird hobby that somehow caught a little wave in cocktail culture. If you bought this book, shared one of my videos, or sent me a photo of a cocktail you created, I am forever grateful for having you along for this journey.

INDEX

PAGE NUMBERS IN ITALICS DENOTE IMAGES.

mustard seeds, 183

N

N₂O chargers
Butterscotch Foam, 121
for foams, 129, 130
Ginger-Infused Tequila, 74
Maple Lemon Foam, 132
Pan Galactic Gargle Blaster, 71
for rapid infusions, 72
navy strength gin, Pan Galactic
Gargle Blaster, 71
Negronis, 152, 179
New York Flip, 96, 97
New York Sour, 96, 138, 139, 164
Nick & Nora glass, 11, 12
nogs, Spiked Eggnog, 98, 99
nutmeg
Glögg (Mulled Wine), 139
Irish Coffee, 102
New York Flip, 96
Pumpkin Spice Syrup, 87
Spiced Apple Cider, 120
Spiked Eggnog, 99

O

Oaxaca Old Fashioned, 60, 61
Office, The, 78
old fashioned glass (rocks glass), 10, 12
Old Fashioned in the Rocks, 149
Old Fashioneds
Benton's Old Fashioned, 124, 125
Classic Old Fashioned, 52, 53
Don Draper's Old Fashioned, 50, 51
Oaxaca Old Fashioned, 60, 61
Pumpkin Spice Syrup in, 87
sweeteners for, 15
Wisconsin Brandy Old Fashioned, 58, 59
Old Smashioned, 151
Old Spanish, 134, 135
Improved, 136, 137
Old Tom gin, Martinez, 29
olive brine, 22, 25
One of Everything, 76, 77
onion powder, 183
orange bitters

Black Manhattan, 38
Classic Gin Martini, 27
Coast-To-Coast, 49
Improved Old Spanish, 136
Martinez, 29
A Song of Ice and Fire, 148
orange juice, 17
Harvey Wallbanger, 111
Samarian Sunset, 166
A Song of Ice and Fire, 148
See also citrus juices
orange peel, flaming, 174
orange twist
Benton's Old Fashioned, 124
Cacao Boulevardier, 75
Oaxaca Old Fashioned, 60
orange wheel
Don Draper's Old Fashioned, 51
Harvey Wallbanger, 111
Wisconsin Brandy Old Fashioned, 59

P

Pam's Green Russian, 63
Pan Galactic Gargle Blaster, 70, 71
peanut butter, 126, 127
Peanut-Butter Infused Bourbon, 126, 127
Peanut Butter Patty (Tagalong) cocktail, 126
peeler, 8, 9
pepper
Bloody Mary, 184
Gordon's Breakfast, 187
Peppermint Patty, 155
peppermint schnapps
Flaming Homer, 169
Peppermint Patty, 155
Perfect Manhattan, 39
Petraske, Sasha, 187
Peychaud's bitters, Inverted Sazerac, 131
Pickleback Shot, 114, 115
pickle brine
Forget-Me-Shot, 113
Pickleback Shot, 114
pickled cocktail onions, 25
pickled jalapeño brine, 183
pickled vegetables, Bloody Mary, 184
pilsner

Bitter Ein Bit, 145
Improved Skittlebrau, 142
pineapple juice, 17
Bitter Ein Bit, 145
Clarified Piña Colada, 68
Pinot Noir, Glögg (Mulled Wine), 139
Pisco Sour, 128
port
Glögg (Mulled Wine), 139
Improved Thanks-Tini, 84
New York Flip, 96
potato vodka, Thanks-Tini, 83
pour-overs
instructions, 104, 104
Manhattan Pour-Over, 105
pousse-café, 163
pressure cooker, 43
proof, 172
Pumpkin Spice Cocktail, 86, 87
Pumpkin Spice Syrup, 87

Q

Q ginger beer, 93

R

Ramazzotti amaro, Maserati, 117
rapid infusions, 72–73, 72, 73
Rea, Andrew, 101
reposado tequila
Flaming Homer, 169
Long Island Iced Tea, 78
Oaxaca Old Fashioned, 60
Spiked Mexican Hot Chocolate, 157
reverse dry shake, 128, 129
rich simple syrup, 15
rocks glass (old fashioned glass), 10, 12
Rowling, J. K., 119
ruby port
Glögg (Mulled Wine), 139
Improved Thanks-Tini, 84
rum
AMF, 81
Clarified Piña Colada, 68
Cuba Libre, 89
Dark 'n Stormy, 93
grapefruit juice with, 17
Improved Cuba Libre, 90
Long Island Iced Tea, 78
One of Everything, 77
Rum Hot Cocoa, 156